REBOOT YOUR LIFE!

BRING BACK YOUR SPARK

LINDA KRAUSS BARNETT

ISBN: 978-1-7352281-0-5 (Paperback)
978-1-7352281-1-2 (eBook)

Turn It Off
Take a few deep breaths
Set a clear intention about what
you want next
And then turn it back on again
Reboot your life

Contents

The Spinning Wheel   1

Turn It Off & Wait   71

Turn It Back On & Reboot Your Life   111

Acknowledgements

Leading up to the writing of this book, many people were a guiding force in my life and all for different reasons. My father taught me to appreciate all of the beauty and magic that this life has to offer. My mom builds my strength and resilience and helps me remember that I am stronger than I can imagine. My husband teaches me to have a sense of humor and laugh no matter how serious things feel. My kids have shown me that my heart can hold infinite amounts of love and that kids are the best teachers in the world. My best friend Patricia Ribeiro Wolfson has been alongside me as my partner in crime as we navigate producing Soul Seekers TV during the duration of writing of this book. Thank you Misti Patrella for your guidance and mentorship in completing this very special debut book. I have had the pleasure of crossing paths with muses and friends that have believed in me and saw the best parts of me when I could not see them in myself. This book is dedicated to all of those that have empowered me with the recipe for making all of my dreams come true.

Prologue: My Beautifully Sad Inspiration For The Title Of This Book

For the first ten years of my teaching career I worked adjacent to my colleague and best friend Anthony Thompson. We would laugh together, inspire each other, learn from each other and be totally silly together. And it made life fun even through the hard times.

We shared so many memories together, but one stands out above the rest. I was (and still am) known as a "Zapper". Any piece of technology that I touched would literally start acting crazy and stop working. So on an almost daily basis, I would run to Tony with my computer in hand and scream, "HELP! It isn't working!" to which he would always reply, "Did you try turning it off and then back on again." Each and every time he said this I would complain about his simplistic response and remind him that it could not possibly be the answer for everything. And yet 99% of the time it was! It almost always worked.

So over time this became our life joke. Whenever we felt stuck or confused or I would just "Zap" things in my life, one of us would stare at the other and ask if they had tried turning it off and then back on. We would laugh at our secret solution to all of life's hardships. In 2016, after months of fighting an aggressive oral cancer, Tony was told by doctors that there was nothing more they could do. We knew the end was near. As I sobbed at his bedside, I told him that I didn't want to teach without him. I told him how lost I was going to feel without him in my life. As he watched the tears and the pain pour from my heart, he leaned over in the bed and whispered in my ear, "It's going to be OK. You have to just turn it back on after I turn off. Just reboot. I will always be here to help."

I used to have the belief that mistakes or roadblocks in life were permanent so I had to be really careful to make as few as possible. I used to feel helpless and powerless to change my circumstances. I have spent hours of my time on Earth regretting past decisions for leading me down the wrong path. I have told a good deal of the world my "If only..." stories.

Historically, I have made fun of the simple solutions offered to my problems. I brushed easy off as a childish suggestion when real answers weren't available. Yet, in that moment at Tony's bedside confronting one of the hardest problems I have ever had to face, he offered me a simple solution. When you are stuck, turn off, wait and then turn back on and reboot. Those words have rattled around in my head ever since.

I sat at my desk one solemn afternoon while writing this book and pondering the zillions of questions running through my brain. What do I title this book? How do I create a program that could help people and make a difference in the world? Why do all of these decisions have to be so hard?

I felt Tony's presence by my side. He once again whispered in my ear and said, "Linda, just reboot." Those words floated through my mind once again as I began to cry. I knew that the easy answer was the right one. I also knew I had the title of my book.

In this book, I will reveal the secret recipe that my best friend Tony and I kept all to ourselves for so many years. No matter where you are in life, no matter what is happening, no matter how bad, or frustrating, or confusing it looks, know that turning things around is always possible. It is possible to get yourself unstuck, to get inspired and take action in your own life.

Join me as I show you the steps I took to give my own life a reboot. I can assure you, I desperately needed one. Once you know it is possible, you'll be able to move through inaction and fear to reboot your own life.

Why I Wrote This Book, And What I Hope You Get Out Of It

Have you ever wished that life worked the same way as technology? If that little spinning rainbow wheel on your computer is going around and around with no end in sight, then all you have to do to fix it is shut it off, wait, and then... tada! Somehow, just that act of shutting it off will make it work perfectly when it is turned back on. Like magic.

Have you wanted to just press the reset button and literally reboot a moment, a period of time, a job, a relationship, any and all things that feel like they aren't working for you? Almost everyone I ask says that they wish they could have a reboot in their own lives. To turn something, or some situation, off and turn it back on again with a fresh and clean perspective. A restart when you feel lost or stuck. This guidebook, based on my own self-discovery and transformation, is your handbook for your own life reboot.

I am sharing my journey through a restart of my own life. In this book I use my stories and experiences to show you that rebooting your life is absolutely possible. If my hot-mess self from a couple years ago could do it, my friend, it is so very possible for you too.

Step by step. With the tips and advice I offer in this guide, it is my hope and prayer that no matter where you find yourself in your own life, that you can pause, reboot, and keep going. No matter how lost you find yourself, there is a way back to YOU.

Welcome to a powerful journey into your own life. Sure, you'll be reading my story, but likely, you'll find yourself in it as well. I am going to share some painful memories. I am doing that so that you know it's possible to turn things around, even if you look in the mirror and don't recognize who you see (which is what happened to me). But, I'm also going to share with you how I found my way back to my own life; how I rebooted my operating system; and upgraded the beliefs that were holding me captive in my own life. I went from unhappy and unfulfilled to hopeful and excited about life. If I can, well then, it's certainly possible for you to do the same.

I want you to know this book is written from my personal perspective. In various parts of the story I refer to God, the Universe, and Source Energy. Those are the words that I use to describe my beliefs and faith. However, as you read, plug in what makes sense for you and your belief system. It is important that it connects to your personal experience.

Journal Prompts. At the end of each section you will find journal prompts. These are there to encourage you to deepen your knowledge of each topic in the section. Please use this as a way to journal your experiences around each main idea. This helps you to go step by step through the reboot process right alongside me. Consider me your guide, and you are reading my story, but you are here to maximize your own reset. It's not enough just to read my story. I want you to use this as a way to dig into your own life.

In the following pages, I have shared the steps I took to reconnect to myself during my own crisis of identity. I'm hoping this book helps you take the steps back to finding your own life reboot. Remember, anything is possible unless you believe it isn't. Let's reboot our lives together. One step at a time.

The Spinning Wheel

The Spinning Wheel

What happens when life is spinning out of control?

You may be trying so hard to improve your life and reclaim your happiness. But if you are anything like me, likely you've been struggling. You may be constantly trying to find happiness, but your sense of disconnect, discomfort and despair remain.

The feeling of spinning out of control is a sign that you are ready for an upgrade. You do not need to know all of the answers to move forward. You need to learn to love yourself again.

This spin is where your journey begins.

Start With The Here And Now
– you are here –

So the adage goes, " in the right place at the right time." I call horse shit. Or at least I used to. When your life is in shambles and you have no idea what to do next, it doesn't feel like that is the best place for you at that moment. In my personal experience, there have been many moments that felt like I was not where I needed to be. I have felt so derailed and off track by life that I wondered if I could ever find my way back. I used to feel isolated and alone, even when I was surrounded by people. I wondered why everyone else in the world knew where they were headed but me. I realized later in life, that many, many people feel off course in their lives. Just like I did.

What I have come to learn is that we all have those moments in life that are wake up calls. These big moments stand out in our memory because they are emotional, and have so much to teach us. Many times, they teach us about love. How to love others. How to love better. And most importantly, how to love yourself. So if that turns out to be

3

true, then could it be that each moment of our life, even when it feels scary, terrible or painful, offers us what we need and maybe not always what we want.

When you see the signs and feel the tug in your heart, maybe these are the little voices of your higher self providing you wisdom and answers to the questions you are seeking. Maybe if you listen more to the voices on the inside instead of always looking for advice from the outside you will be able to make choices that are aligned with your most authentic and joyful self.

When you figure out that your life isn't the way it is because you are bad, or that there is something wrong with you, but that you are simply spinning, lost or stuck on your path, you begin the amazing search of finding your true heart and soul. The path that is speaking to your biggest dreams and cannot be dimmed by your biggest fears. The path that this lifetime is meant for you to walk on.

Join me as I retrace my steps from losing my worth, to finding the life that I was meant to live. In this book, I'm sharing the steps I took that helped me go from feeling overwhelmed with sadness and hopelessness, to finding my soul's purpose. I want you to know that it's completely possible for you too. Hopefully, my journey will help you travel from darkness to light. From lost to found. To your own life reboot.

Realizing That You Are Spinning
– it's not pretty –

You are here! And so was I. I was spinning in thoughts of confusion and doubt and even a sense of great despair. We have all experienced these bitter moments of our lowest point. My story starts right there. The exact spot in my life when my world was rocked so hard that I could actually feel the Earth spinning on its axis. I call it the Big Dipper, because it felt like it was a big dip in my life when the stars did not align. If you have ever been through tough times or trauma such as losing a job, getting a divorce, or grief of any kind, then you know what a big low can feel like. The truth is, that it doesn't even have to be a life changing event. Sometimes we can feel low from depression or anxiety that feels outside of our control. Whatever you call it when hitting a huge wall and feeling as if life is beating you down, I think we can all agree that it feels like total shit.

I'm talking about the moment when you look in the mirror, or hear the sound of your voice and think, "Who the hell is that woman?" I can tell you, that the moment I looked into the mirror and saw a stranger staring back at me was the moment that I realized I was lost. It was definitely my Big Dipper moment.

It is important to trace your steps back to the time when you lost sight of who and what you really are. You don't have to stay there long. It's not necessary to dwell in it. Just check in with yourself long enough to figure out what happened. Then you can adjust. Make different choices. Create something even more fulfilling.

I know what it is like to feel off-course. I mean completely lost. So lost, you aren't sure who you are anymore. Or even scarier, how to find your way back to you. It wasn't quite a depression, but it also wasn't far off. For me, the worst part of being that lost was not knowing how I got there. I had no idea what the hell I should do to find myself again. What is the next right step when you feel paralyzed with doubt and desperation?

In my case, I was lost inside of a life that read like the script of a blockbuster Hollywood movie. An actual movie, really. My husband traveled around the world doing special effects for the movie business. We lived (and still do) in a beautiful home in Florida. The kids and I travel with my husband when the kids are out of school. In the beginning, it sounded truly glamorous. But the truth is that it wasn't. I was very unhappy, and my only solution was to place blame everywhere I could except for myself.

I didn't start out as a reactionary, angry person. When I was younger, I was a woman on fire. I believed everything was possible. Most of all, I believed in myself. What I've come to realize is that I didn't lose myself in one moment. It was in a series of moments, and choices, that seemed to happen slowly, over a period of time that led me to spin out of control.

The disconnection to my identity and purpose started spiraling when I left my first career in the movie business. I quit the industry after a decade so that I could focus on building our family and creating a home for our children. This was also the same time that I stopped doing all of the things that selfishly made me feel young, free, and happy. Instead, I started doing all of the grown-up "shoulds". In exchange for traveling with no home base, I should create a home and lay down some roots for my children. In exchange for a freelance job with no consistent income, I should get a more stable job with steady pay. I should only do the things that support my husband and kids. In the name of should, responsibility and stability, I took all of the fun out of my life. That created an unhappiness and resentment that started to build and build until I was in a personal prison of my own making.

Fast forward 5 years to my biggest dip of all. I can very clearly remember the day that I hit my lowest point. Some would call it a midlife crisis but I realized that it was actually more of an identity crisis.

Let me paint the picture for you. My husband and I are standing outside in the darkness of our backyard. I was cornering him late at night to ensure that the kids were sleeping and couldn't hear us. I was doing this so that I could beg him to just see me. I wanted him to need me and desire me like he used to when we first met.

He gave me a bewildered look like he wasn't quite sure how to respond to what I was asking of him. I could tell he was looking through me and almost past me to a place where he might be able to escape this situation. Maybe he was looking for a secret portal to take him away from the desperate thralls of a screaming and crazed wife into the serenity of a far away place. I am sure if his brain was wired to a projector, it would have read, "GET ME THE HELL OUT OF HERE! THIS WOMAN IS CRAZY." And at that moment, he was right.

And you know what? This wasn't our first rodeo. We had been here before. I knew that by this point, he was already tuning me out like a bad TV channel. Resolution on this night didn't seem to be an option, so at this point the best thing I could do was save myself from anymore desperate and clingy behavior. I decided to go back inside and show him that I could tune him out too. We had perfected the tit for tat.

And then the worst thing happened. As if that moment was not already one of the worst of my life, it dipped farther. As I walked away from my husband on that terrible night, I caught a reflection of myself in the kitchen windows. That was when the shit really hit the fan.

This moment will forever be ingrained in my mind

because it stopped me in my tracks. I did not know the woman staring back at me in the glass. My reflection seemed unrecognizable. No matter how hard I looked, I couldn't see myself.

The woman staring back at me was heavier, angrier and more resentful than I had ever been, surely. She had dark circles under her eyes, and looked old and exhausted. She had tears streaming down her face and a defeated look deep inside her eyes. Who the hell was this woman? This was not the woman that I wanted to be when I was a little girl. How had I grown up to be this? I did not love this woman in any way. My heart was consumed with a disdain for who I was, and who I had allowed myself to become.

My biggest desire at that moment was to banish this woman to a faraway tower where I would never have to see her again. I closed my eyes to shut out the horrifying image of myself. I turned and walked away in complete defeat.

If you've ever felt as lost as I was at this moment in my life, you'll likely empathize with my intense despair. I was seriously questioning the idea that I had literally become invisible to the world. In reality, the only person I was invisible to was myself.

I had so many important jobs that I believed gave me value. I was a mother, a wife, a teacher, a daughter, a friend... How could I be so present with these roles, and be completely absent for myself? People needed me to do things for them and to be there for them. To make their lives easier. To make them happy. When it came to what I wanted and needed - no one seemed to care, especially not me. And now, I could no longer ignore it. The woman I had become was challenging the very existence of the woman I was once was and longed to be again.

Things had not been going well for a while in my marriage. My husband was away a lot. He came home looking to recharge his battery with a house full of smiles and good times. In contrast, I was looking forward to his time home to recharge my tired and empty battery. I envisioned a doting husband who filled in every ounce of loneliness I had felt in his absence.

Not being on the same page when he came home was not contributing to a happy reunion. I was beginning to understand how any woman could get the reputation as a "ball and chain." I was literally holding my husband captive in all of my insecurities. As soon as he got home, I started piling them on him. Which in turn, made him want to run away and leave again.

It was around this time that my ego began to dictate its masterpiece of fiction to me. I took diligent notes as any faithful student would. What it was saying wasn't new. In fact, it was as cruel as ever. The thoughts racing through my mind were weaving a story that confirmed all of my doubts and fears. My story was that I had become undesirable and unlovable and that my destiny would be one of loneliness and solitude. The story I was telling myself was to brace my heart and mind for the imminent rejection that was headed my way.

Standing conscious in that moment of awareness of what I had become, filled me with a deep sadness. A sadness I had rarely felt before. One thing was for sure, I was not going to spend the rest of my life as this version of myself. I didn't want to be the angry woman staring back at me in that window. But the toughest questions of all were swirling around and around in my mind.

Fight, Flight Or Freeze
– survive vs. thrive –

Fight, flight or freeze are the three human responses to fear or trauma. "Between stimulus and response there is a space. In that space is our power to choose our response. In our response lies our growth and our freedom." Victor Frankl's quote here is a perfect discussion of that space, right before you decide which choice you will make. How YOU will respond to what is happening in your life.

Up until this point in my life I had used these very primitive brain reactions to get me out of all of the tough situations I'd faced. If fight, flight or freeze were the go-to defenses that I had available then I was not left with many choices that were guided by my soul or heart. I was just constantly in reaction mode. All of my tactics were based on a limited operating system that did not use creativity, passion, or purpose to fuel my responses to stress.

Flight has always been one of my favorite forms

14

of protection in my intimate relationships. I have always used escape as the way to handle things that scared and intimidated me. When I felt the slightest bit threatened, off I would go as far away from the situation as humanly possible. When conversations or confrontations don't go the way I want them to, I used to find that walking out and away was the best way to protect my heart from breaking. The reality is that you sometimes need to tell your ego to settle down while you sit in the moment and face the fears that come your way.

Some of my most powerful answers have come in the moments that I have resisted the urge to flee. When my husband and I fight, I want to run away. But, when I can stay, relax, be calm, and talk to him about what is arising for me, and listen when he talks...well, that's actually when the real transformation takes place. Not in the response. The answers come in staying present - even when I really want to run away. (I'm still working on this now. It's a lifetime practice.)

There is so much information available when you get curious about your discomfort, instead of running from it, fighting it, or pretending it doesn't exist. It may feel very uncomfortable at the moment, but remember, feelings are like waves. They are not permanent. The idea is to ride the wave of how you are feeling with curiosity, instead of resistance or fear. If you can watch your feelings come in, and then wash back out again, as you would watch a wave in the ocean, you don't need to become reactionary. You can become the observer.

Again, when I do this, instead of reacting to how I feel, the results are always life changing. Let's go back to the example of my husband. I am usually not listening much to what he is trying to tell me because I am already planning what I will say next. I'm already not present, and technically, I'm moving into the fight response. Anyone know what I am talking about? But, when I allow myself to be more compassionate, and truly hear what he is trying to communicate, then I find myself feeling softer and more willing to love. I can then come at him from the perspective of love versus fear. This changes the whole conversation.

I was not always this clear on how to deal with my fears. Years ago I would have handled it with my usual panic attack. They started when I was a young girl but in my mid twenties they started to consume me. Like an unwanted guest, they would appear out of nowhere and fill me with a fear so powerful that my heart would race while at the same time my breath would disappear.

From the time I was about 6 years old I remember having such terrible panic attacks that I would keep a brown paper bag on my nightstand. I would wake up in the middle of the night hyperventilating, convinced that I was going to die because I could not breathe. These attacks diminished for the most part as I got older. Until I reached my early twenties. Then they came back with a vengeance.

Although my panic attacks had started again several years before meeting my husband, he seemed to have the magic potion for helping me to work through it. Many years ago, while we were at home watching football, I had one of the worst panic attacks of my life. My panic got even worse because I was adding on my fear that this man with whom I was in a new relationship, would assume I was crazy and want no part in it. Instead what happened was in that moment, he stepped in and just knew what to do. I knew we were on a lifetime journey together.

He ran a bath. I stepped in, and was surprised when he joined me. He gently held me close and told me to close my eyes while he guided me to visualize the water drawing all of the negative thoughts and energy away from my body. Then as he drained the water, he made me imagine that it was taking all of the anxiety down the drain. Leaving me with only my own bright white light. I knew in that moment that he was my person. Instead of judging me for what I thought was one of my greatest flaws, he embraced me with love and sensitivity. He proved that he was committed to being my partner through thick and thin. He helped me move through one of the scariest moments of my life with certainty that it was all going to be ok. I needed that. I needed him.

How Did I Get Here?
– where did I go wrong? –

So now, back to my lowest point. Remember, I had just had a fight with my husband, and then I saw what looked like a stranger in the window outside. But, unfortunately, it really was me. I walked inside to take a hot shower and clear my mind. I didn't know what else to do. Maybe I could wash all of this away.

I realized on my way to the shower that this felt familiar. Unfortunately, my husband and I had literally had this same, exact argument many times before. It always followed the same script. I begged to be an object of his desire. He played deaf. He feared losing me more than he longed to escape me. I forgave him because loving him poorly seemed better than losing him all together. And back to the beginning and around again. The only thing that ever changed about the scene was the venue.

I was living on a loop. How do you break a pattern like that? How do I stop it? I felt powerless.

Power-less was an accurate way to shed light on my circumstance. I felt less power than I ever had before.

I was telling myself a doozy of a story. This well-crafted fiction was that my husband traveled all the time. He was doing exciting things all day long, while I was trudging through the mud. I was convinced that he was seeing young and beautiful women at work. He was then forced to come home to a woman that stopped loving herself, and could not see her own beauty. These thoughts, and stories just kept circulating in my head. Worst of all, I was holding him responsible for these made up stories.

While he was off living the good life (or so I was telling myself) I was stuck in my status quo raising two children with a full-time job, and very little time for any kind of acceptable form of self-care. I was an elementary school teacher giving my all to small children during the day to help mold their hearts and minds. I was single parenting on most days and I had a house full of chores to maintain. I was doing nothing to nurture the woman I was because of my devotion to the other more important roles that I had to play in the movie of my life. Each of those choices I made, in the name of love, was another choice away from counting myself as being important. Each time I made myself insignificant, I took another step into the land of lost, unhappy and frustrated.

I mean, isn't that what a good mother does? We take care of others at the expense of ourselves. Isn't selflessness a better option than selfishness? Isn't that what we've always been taught? So...basically, I was not to blame for any of this! Obviously. I was busy trying to be a great mom and wife and teacher. It's just that somewhere along the way, I lost a woman I once knew named "Linda."

Is she gone forever? Or is there a dream of getting her back? "When?" was all I could think. Or even scarier, "How?"

I had heard people tell me not to worry. Many women told me that being a mom would get easier. That I would find my way. And in the motherhood department, it certainly did get a bit easier as they got a little older. But despite all of my hard work, I still felt like an alien visiting my own life.

But the question that kept rearing its ugly head to be answered was always the same: how did I get here?

Where To Start When You Feel Lost

– time to face yourself –

This was not the first time I felt lost. When I dug deep into my memories I saw event after event where I took on that it was better to play small. That it was not important to talk about the truth. It is important to keep quiet. In fact, I had been here many times before.

Really, the feelings of deep loss were not new to me. There have been many difficult times in my life. When I was young and dealt with sexual abuse, I felt lost. When I had to keep it quiet for years to protect people I knew, I felt lost. I felt lost when my childhood best friend called me to tell me we wouldn't see each other again because they were moving away. Our friendship was gone in an instant. I felt lost when my parents divorced. I was in college and really needed my family's support the most. I felt lost when I was holding my father's hands feeling them go cold moments after he took his last breath. When my hero and

23

first love left this physical world, I felt the most lost and alone that I had ever felt before. I felt lost when my mother was diagnosed with breast cancer. I felt lost watching her suffer from the burns of radiation.

I felt lost when the man with whom I had been best friends and taught with for a decade, (the same guy who gave me the inspiration for the title of this book!) announced that he had terminal cancer. I sat with him at the doctor's appointment listening to them tell him that his chances of survival were not very good. I felt lost when he cried and told me that he wished we had more time together.

All of these losses were very different. The most important thing is that they all had one component in common: I was not the fundamental cause of the problem. I simply had to manage through these situations.

Yet in that moment with my husband in the backyard, this loss felt different. This was a whole new level of lost and invisible. The difference this time was that I was not the innocent victim, but rather the actual cause.

I knew deep down that I was the root of my own demise. I had no idea what to do to fix me. To fix our relationship. I felt like I was getting sucked into a black hole with no way out. All I could do was crawl into bed, bury myself under my covers, and go to sleep.

The next morning I woke up before the sun, and before my family. Although I usually find it relaxing when I'm the first one up, there was no way I could sit still long enough to enjoy today's silence. I chose to work through this situation in the way that felt the most comfortable to me. I started writing.

I took out one of my many journals from my large collection. I have always loved the possibilities that lay upon the blank pages. Anything could be written. A new story was always possible.

I selected the one whose cover read, DREAM BIG to LIVE BIG. I will remember the cover of that journal for the rest of my life. It's imprinted in my mind because very important words were transcribed inside of it on that day. I flipped open the notebook and waited for the words I needed to say.

It took a moment, and then finally one little but mighty sentence floated in.

"I AM LOST! PLEASE HELP ME TO FIND MYSELF AGAIN!"

I picked up my pen and looked down at what I wrote. I started to cry. Those words were the most real and honest I had been with myself in a long time. I sat there for a second, staring down at a mostly empty but very poignant page.

As I sat in silence, I had some big questions start bubbling up. How in the name of all that is holy did I get myself here? How do I find my way back? Where was back? Back to what? Will I ever be me again? Who am I really?

And what the hell happened to, "Ask and you shall receive?" All I was doing was asking. Nonstop. Without pause. Where were my answers?! What I would soon realize is that the Universe was not going to just hand them over. My assistance would come in a different way.

It felt like the Linda that I had known all of my life was gone. I went into the bathroom to see if

I could see any of the old me in the mirror. Were there any parts of me left? This new one in her place was no one that I recognized. She was certainly not someone I wanted to spend the rest of my life with. And yet... here we were, staring back at each other in the mirror as enemies that were bound by sharing one body and mind. How did I go from my young, empowered and full-of-life self, to this? What had I done to deserve this?

Then I felt a deep longing for connection to my past self. I missed that girl in her 20's that loved singing and dancing until the sun came up. I was the woman that didn't take shit from anyone. I knew my worth back then, and loved myself so much. I needed no approval. It was a fabulous time. I felt strong. Confident.

I needed her to come back. This was non-negotiable.

It's Okay Not To Be Okay
– just don't stay there forever –

Is it ever okay to NOT be okay? I'm serious. Think about it. Does the world give us permission to not be okay? Is it ever acceptable to be down, sad, upset, angry or any of the "lower" emotions? Isn't there a time limit for how long it is acceptable to not be okay?

When I couldn't find the right tools to begin excavating my inner being from the ravine it had fallen into, I had to analyze what options were left. As I continued my hunt for the answers I found my unexpected next step in a conversation with my mom.

We were sitting in my kitchen one day. She once again had to witness her daughter deeply sighing in defeat. She looked me gently in the eyes. I braced myself for yet another one of her famous, "get your shit together" speeches. But instead, she proceeded to talk to me in a way that touched me to my core.

What she said went something like this, "Linda, when you are sick and your body is aching you often have to take medicine to get better. So you go to the store and get the medicine and come home ready to take it. Unfortunately though, the pills are huge and you hate swallowing them. So even though you know they will help, you procrastinate the inevitable because you are avoiding the discomfort and bad taste of swallowing them down. But Linda, all you have to do is take the medicine. Actually swallow it, and then be patient. Wait for it to take effect. In the meantime, it is okay to rest and take care of yourself. That's what helps the medicine work." Again, this felt very reminiscent of the concept of a REBOOT.

We both knew the medicine she was talking about was self-love, responsibility and happiness. She was right. I hadn't been taking care of me. My mom was trying to lead me down the path of confidence. I just wasn't sure I was ready to follow.

How was I supposed to take care of myself? How was I supposed to take the medicine if I spent all of my awake time tending to what everyone else needed first? I had so many questions. And, I have to say, I was a little frustrated. But, I could tell that what she said was already burrowing into my heart. Even if I had no idea how it would surface yet.

One would think that having had these realizations would begin to shift things in my life right away. Nothing could be further from the truth. Nothing changed for quite a while. Even after I realized that I was lost, it took me a while to sit in it and stew before any meaningful action took place. I had to take a while to wrap my brain around the concept of what it meant to be unable to identify with who I had become. That was scary. I needed to wallow in the realization that I was clearly in the midst of an identity crisis.

By definition, according to Merriam-Webster, an identity crisis is, "a period of uncertainty and confusion in which a person's sense of identity becomes insecure, typically due to a change in their expected aims or role in society." That about summed it up for me. Frankly, being where I was at the moment was really my only choice. I had no idea what to do to fix my situation. I didn't want to fight, run from or deny what was happening. For the moment, I had to be okay, not being okay.

As with many deep personal epiphanies that we have in life, they don't typically rise to the surface overnight. They certainly do not dissolve overnight. So, like my mom advised, I took the uncomfortable medicine that was being offered, and I waited. I waited for the answers to come.

My usual practice when I wait for clarity and discernment is to journal it out. I have a way I do it each time. At the top of each page I write my question. Then I would free-write about the question. For example:

- Why is my relationship with my husband such a struggle?
- Where was I taught that to be a good mother meant to sacrifice your happiness?
- Why am I so unhappy?

After a great deal of self-reflection and journaling, some nuggets of insight began to surface in my writing. Finally! What I found is that many of these limiting beliefs that I was feeling had an origin. Somewhere along the way I was taught (most of us were) that there were certain rules that we use to play the game of life. One of the places I was handed down this belief was from my mother. It's not her fault. I don't blame her.

She learned it from her mother, and her mother before her, and so on down the lineage of the history of women. I think many women who have kids can agree with what I am saying. Shoot, you do not even need to have kids for this stupid belief to show up. The lie we have been taught is that being a woman, and even more a mother, requires tremendous sacrifice and selflessness. We are shown that everyone else's needs must be met before our own. But guess what ladies... It's bullshit!

When I was a little girl I remember vividly hearing my mother talk about the things she wished she could have done and accomplished. She had to hold back on most of them due to her responsibilities to our family. Since she was a good mother to me, it confirmed that her devotion to the job was well done. Armed with a belief that was now tattooed into the programming of my mind, I took this as a rite of passage into my own motherhood. I really wanted to earn the title of "worthy mom." I too would need to put myself last while everyone and everything else came first. It was what I "should do."

Yet, as I practiced this ridiculous ritual in my own

life I found myself so surprised at the outcome. I was doing what it took to be a "good mom." But for some reason, even though it seemed like I was doing it right, it made me feel all kinds of wrong. I was so unhappy!

How could eons of generations of women manage through this? How could so many women live by a principle that had so many flaws and made you feel terrible? I knew that being a mother was the greatest blessing of my life. Somehow I did not get the memo from the other moms that me being a mom entailed killing the dreams of the woman I was before children.

But when I look back and reflect on the relationship I had with my mom growing up, I can see where she might have been affected by it too. There were many times where she was far away and distracted. She was nervous and stressed and sometimes unavailable emotionally. Then there were times that she was the life of the party and inspired me with her smile. The times that she was the best mom was when she was the happiest.

I began to ponder these memories as I watched

myself repeating the same behaviors in my own life. I was trying to hydrate those I love from an empty cup. My empty cup. I can tell you clearly that my cup was definitely not full. I felt depleted. Not exactly a plan for success. The result was that my family and I were all parched for joy, laughter, and fun. I had unknowingly contributed to that.

It was clear that I needed to find a way to break this pattern of dysfunctional motherhood. It was time to shake things up. I needed a reboot. You should know that one of my goals is that this book will help to squash that toxic version of parenting. It's time to end that shit.

Choosing Responsibility Over Blame

– no more blame game –

What is most important to note is that at this point I was blaming all of my not-enough-ness on other people. Namely my husband. Looking at it now, my self-esteem was actually in the shitter. I was afraid my husband didn't want me. I could not comprehend that my body, that was once home to two babies, could still look and feel sexy to him. I wasn't sure I could still be beautiful despite more wrinkles, a few stretch marks and a more curvaceous body. I didn't feel worthy of love.

Because I couldn't face myself, my husband became the target of my insecurities. I was sure that he was the cause of my rock bottom. Or at least that was the story I was telling myself over and over and over again. It seemed to serve my needs to evade responsibility for my own life. It's just easier to make any other person the bad-guy.

As I began to dream about how to dig myself out

of my massive identity crisis, I was gleaning all the places I wanted to make my situation about other people. I wanted to blame everyone else for my misery. I mean, I *really* wanted to. It felt better to blame someone else than take responsibility for the mess I had created.

As you may know from your own personal experiences, it is so much easier to blame someone else. It's not always easy to see how much of a part we have to play in what happens in our lives. It is very difficult to see your own behavior objectively, and to own it.

Once you do, it gets more uncomfortable, not less. It can sometimes be painful to witness what you have said and done to yourself and others. Blame is easy because we can see the actions and flaws in others so much easier than those in ourselves.

> This person made me feel sad.
> This person made me feel unloved.
> This person hurt me.

It may in fact be true that someone did something that was painful to you. That most certainly does happen. But in the end, if you allowed it again, and again, and again, you were a contributor to the situation as well. By allowing someone else's shitty behavior toward you, you are saying, "Yes. This is acceptable in my life."

This point is not easy to accept. "It is hard to see the color of your own eyes," as they say. I could easily have blamed my traveling husband for me feeling lonely. Or to blame my mom for setting me up for unhappiness. Or, I could have blamed myself for having needs. It would have felt great. For a long time, I did. Unfortunately, it wasn't solving anything, and it was creating all kinds of suffering. For everyone.

People would always ask where my husband was. When I answered with "This time he is in..." I would usually get the same response. "Awww. That must be so hard for you with two kids. I am so sorry. If you need anything let me know!"

They felt sorry for my life. That extra boost of pity from others gave me the permission I needed to to slack in my own life. Obviously, anyone could have seen that my life was hard as shit. By blaming my husband, or anyone else I could think of, I took all responsibility away from myself.

I was so good at blaming others for my life, that I kept going. When I complained about the weight slowly stacking on my body, my blame game continued. I would complain that it was impossible for me to get to the gym with two small children in tow. My very good friends gave me the sympathy I craved yet again, "Awww. I totally get it. That must be so hard!"

Thus my excuses continued. I was too exhausted by the time I was done with work, and the house, and the kids to do anything for myself. These things obviously just were not my fault.

I had pretty much convinced myself that my problems had nothing to do with me. It was not my fault my marriage was crumbling, my finances were shot, my weight was out of control, my health was dwindling, my exhaustion was debilitating... not my fault...Not MY Fault! NOT MY FAULT!

Now it was time to be honest with myself. I had made each choice. At the end of the day, I am the one that decided not to go to the gym. I decided not to take care of myself. I decided to put everyone else's needs ahead of my own. Every reason I gave myself was nothing more than an excuse to hide behind. So, really, who was to blame, but me?

Shit.

Saving Yourself Is An Inside Job
– only you can do it –

Good or bad I could no longer remain in denial. I could no longer ignore my situation. I now saw where I really was. If you've had to face yourself, and take an honest review of your life, you also understand how difficult it can be to take responsibility for your choices - even when you thought you didn't have any. That is not easy to see. (If you are starting to look at your choices at this point, I honor you.) However, in my case, the only way to get over it was to go through it. So I had to face it. The lies I had been telling myself became obvious and I needed to face them head on.

1. I had a mindset based on fear that was no longer serving me.
2. I had gifts, talents, and skills that I was not claiming.
3. I felt powerless to shift my perspective.
4. I spent years blaming the world for the issues of my life.
5. I took very little responsibility for my failures.

So here was the bottom line: at any age and at any phase we can start again and reboot.

I had been a martyr for too long. I gave my power away to others and left myself feeling powerless as a result. Clearly the world had done this to me. I was not to blame for all the shit I had accumulated. I was just trying to survive. Isn't that what humans are designed to do? This story was no longer serving me either. It was coming time to shut it down.

At some point in adulthood, I bought into the fairy tale that it was someone else's job to rescue me from my mess. You should know, that is the exact thing I went around saying I would never do when I was in my twenties. I was the righteous girl that swore I would not relinquish my power to a man. I knew deep in my bones that I was fully capable of standing on my own two feet. Yet here I was, just waiting in my tower, locked away until someone else would do their part to save me.

My Rapunzel fantasy wasn't working. I just didn't quite know how to rescue myself yet. But unlike Rapunzel, no prince charming, or ogre, or any other male hero was looking for the job of being my lifesaver. That was sending me over the edge. Waiting for my husband to save me from myself was getting old. It wasn't working.

The more I thought of alternative solutions, the more frightened I became. The answers were right in front of my face. I just didn't know if I had the inner strength to face it. Saving myself was going to be much more difficult than I had anticipated. Even worse than waiting for someone else to do it, was realizing that it has to come from you. There was no way around the realization that I was my own savior. It seemed as if this was turning out to be an inside job and that scared the hell out of me.

You Are The Director Of Your Own Life Movie
– make it one you love –

Night after night my husband would call me from his location on set and tell me about his day or his week. He would share his adventures about all of the awesome things that were happening, or retell stories with excitement about the parties he had been to and all of the people that he met. He saw it as sharing parts of himself with me. I saw it as bragging about the kind of life he had without me in it.

Oppositely, my stories consisted of my days filled with kids both at work and at home. Sometimes I would even get to tell him that I had managed to stay awake past nine. It felt like I was the boring one, and he got to have all of the fun. If I'm being honest with myself, I could have gone out too. I could have afforded a babysitter. I had great friends. My husband never stopped me from having a life. But, partying when you feel tired, unattractive, and empty does not sound too great either.

I knew change was coming. I could feel it. Things couldn't keep going on like they were. My husband and I were starting to drift even further apart and I was starting to get nervous that we might not come back together. So, I made a decision. I was going to take a stand in my life and fight for my marriage. I was going to have to step into the hero role and come face to face with myself. That takes courage!

If you will recall, my first career was in the movie business. You get used to all of the main archetypes that people fall into in movies. For women, there is the leading lady, the best friend, the goddess, the muse. Sometimes you are the hero, sometimes the villain. I realized that I had most definitely not been the hero in my own life.

It was time to look at the script that I had been writing for far too long and change the story. I wanted the lead of my movie to be smart and strong. I wanted her to be a woman that would empower other women and lead by example. Up to this point, I was not playing the lead of my movie. Instead I felt more like a supporting character in a movie about myself. Have you ever felt that way about your life?

I had been allowing my mind to feast on complete crap for years! All of my problems had an excuse, but not one good reason. They were obviously not my fault.

No more! It was time to look into my eyes and truly see me again. If I was going to change my role in my movie, I was going to have one last conversation with my old self.

The Old Script

- I am lonely because my traveling husband goes off to work and leaves me all alone.
- I am unhealthy because I am too exhausted to workout and eat healthy.
- I have no energy to take a shot at my real dreams.
- I am broke because I was taught to live in lack and scarcity.

My New Lines

- I have a husband who works very hard to

support our family and that sometimes takes him out of town.

- So when he comes home, we make the most out of the precious time we spend together.
- I ask for help when I need it and that allows me the opportunity to make time to care for my mind and body.
- Abundance is my birthright and I am learning to care for money so that it will care for me.
- I am enough!

My old script for life was never going to work. It was already terribly unsuccessful. Ultimately, it is no one else's job to fix me. It is no one else's job to fix you either. If you want to create something else, to have a life that is different than the one you have now, it will take facing you and your life with honesty, compassion and love.

Just like I did.

Your turn.

You Are Not A Victim
– make new choices to get new results –

It is not an easy process to accept responsibility for a life gone awry. It is most certainly not easy to empower yourself with the ability to stand in your own greatness if you aren't in the habit of doing it. I spent too long looking for the answers outside of myself. As soon as I was able to see that blame's rightful place was at my own doorstep, then I was also able to take back control of my life. I could now steer myself in the direction of all the things I have ever wished for or desired.

For so long, I felt like an insect stuck inside a spider's web. I couldn't move forward, and I couldn't go back. It felt like I was stuck until I would be swallowed whole. Part of me was terrified. Part of me felt relief from having to figure out how to untangle myself from my predicament.

Isn't life like that? The natural force of momentum can feel difficult to shift. Just like piling on weight is easier than losing it. Making a mess is much easier than cleaning it up. For most of us, spending money is easier than making it. Of course, staying stuck can be much easier than actually figuring out how to move forward.

I had recited my excuses so many times that they had become memorized. I had automatic answers for anyone who dared to ask me about marriage, weight, or work. Those answers always solicited sympathy. That worked just fine for me.

Well, until that night in the backyard with my husband it had been working...

*__Please Note__: I write this section gently, because this is not meant as victim shaming. If you've been through something serious, please know that in so many ways, I completely understand. Some things happen outside of our control. I am only attempting to illuminate our beliefs around the things in our life that we have the power to change. Which in my personal belief is almost anything. Even when we can't control what happens to us, we are usually in control of how we use it to shape our lives.

Real Change Requires Self-Love
– oh dear –

There was still a lot left to figure out if I was going to turn things around. However, one thing that I did know for sure was that the status quo was no longer working for me. The status quo of allowing my thoughts to stay in doubt, negativity, insecurity, jealousy and self-loathing were ruining my life. Literally. So...now what? I needed new thoughts.

I knew that I couldn't continue to blame my husband, or anyone else for the problems of my life anymore. Even though I really wanted to. I also knew that I wasn't fooling anyone by pretending to hold it all together even though it was actually all falling apart.

What was my brilliant plan? How was I going to fix this and save me and my family? You want to know my secret? I had no plan. But, I knew what my next steps needed to be.

I knew I needed to be honest with myself, and face

some hard truths. I needed to show up authentically. I needed to take responsibility for my life and the issues that were causing my sadness. And, I needed to find out how to stop hating myself.

So, like anyone who has a need, but doesn't know where to start, I went to the internet. I watched half of YouTube looking for some clarity. I kept hearing the same word over and over again: mindset. It was a buzz-word that was being thrown around quite a bit in these videos. What I would soon understand was how much my own negative mindset was actually affecting my life.

This idea seemed like such a powerful tool for other people, so I decided to try it on for myself and see if it would work for me. People kept advertising that if you change your mindset, you can change your life. So, that seemed like the magic pill. I did have mean self-talk. I wasn't very nice to myself. My thoughts were constant reminders of all my flaws. I would never talk to another person that way. But, why was I talking that way to myself? How do you go about changing the conversation inside your head? Is it one of those fake-it-until-you-make-it kind of things?

Do I just decide to change it, and then, *poof* new mindset?

I tried a whole bunch of times to, "think loving thoughts" about myself and, "be positive." But it just didn't last. Frankly, I didn't believe it. It didn't feel real. It felt like something I was just saying to myself. I was realizing that the fake-it-till-you-make-it mindset work was not working for me.

What I really learned here - the bottom line - from all of these videos is that truly loving myself was going to be required for me to change. To change my mindset. To change my life. I needed to find a way to feel that love for myself in my heart. It had to feel real. But how do I love myself?

I started in the only place I've always felt love no matter what. I started with my kids. There is nothing that makes me feel more incredible than when one of my kids looks at me with all of the love in the world. They stare at me with wide-eyed wonder and tell me how much they love me. In those moments I absolutely do believe that I am enough.

So I started there. I allowed myself to search for the greatness in me that my kids saw. It felt so great to see myself from the eyes of love, that I slowly looked for other areas where that love was also present. In my mother's eyes. In a big hug from friends. Every once in a while, I could still feel it in the touch of my husband's hands.

What I realized here, and I've been sharing with you up until now (this is big and I want you to pay close attention) is that I had been focusing on the lack of love in my life. Not the love that was around me all of the time. I had just been focusing my attention in the wrong places. As soon as I shifted to the places where I was feeling loved, it felt better. So, I kept doing it. And I kept finding more love. That was how I started the process of loving myself.

Woman On A Mission
– change feels good! –

It felt so good to start loving myself more, that I wanted to keep looking for places where I may have missed the signs of love. I was ready to start changing things. I started looking for love in all areas of my environment. I began by making better food choices with the meals I was cooking. I was choosing to wear bright clothing that made me feel happy. I rearranged the furniture in my living room to feel less stagnant. Little by little these changes were bringing a smile to my face and causing me to change my perspective on the day to day monotony.

Change became my mission! I started paying attention to any solution that the universe was offering. In an ironic twist that most of my friends didn't understand at the time, I signed up to be a rep of a skincare line. I heard about it from a fellow movie wife. She hooked me by saying this could be a way for our husbands to halt their traveling lifestyle.

It felt like maybe this would be a way to solve my problem! Sell skincare, make a ton of money, retire my husband and cure my loneliness. Sounds easy enough, right?

My friends were surprised because they knew I was not big on sales in any way, shape, or form. I was especially terrible at selling something I was not passionate about. It did not take long to realize this was just another failed plan. It felt like I was taking one step forward, two steps back.

However, there were some benefits. My short time with this company exposed me to a plethora of personal development and coaching videos from their top leaders. This would ultimately lead me to my biggest transformation so far.

Unexpectedly, those mind-expanding videos were like the magical breadcrumbs that began to shift my mindset and get me excited about my life again. Watching those videos, by myself, in the dark, while my family was asleep is where I planted my feet in the mud of my life. I was 100% committed to trudging my way back to me.

I watched those videos and felt tinges of excitement

and inspiration that I hadn't felt in years. Decades even. I heard things that lit a match in the dark chambers of my soul. It felt like I had revealed the light within me, to finally be able to escape the darkness that was closing in around me.

What was it that was so magical? So transformative? What did I hear that changed my life?

I was reminded again and again, by expert after expert that I am a co-creator in my life. Let me explain what I mean by co-creator. Every moment allows you the opportunity for choice. Whether the thing that happened to you is something that you like or not. You have the free will ability to choose how you respond to that situation. Most of us forget that. These videos were reminding me that I was not a victim in my life. I can take what I am given by life, and believe it. Or, I can take what I am given by life, and decide to create something different. That is what makes you a co-creator. This is how you work in partnership with the Universe/God/Source/Spirit.

Let me say this again. At every moment. You are the co-creator of your life.

I was learning that shifting my mindset was possible. I could actually, and intentionally go from believing that I wasn't good enough, to feeling worthiness and self-love. It was exactly what I needed. (Why didn't I learn this in school?!) That was the next step to repair this mess with my husband.

If I could continue the momentum of feeling hopeful and inspired then couldn't I steer this ship in a different direction? I had been stuck believing that I was too old for a new beginning. That everything was already set. I had already made my decisions in life. I was now being reminded that I could still choose. I could choose what I wanted to be and do in this lifetime at any time.

Oh wow! Once I lit that fire in my heart, I could not get enough of the inspiration. I was a woman on a mission. I consumed video after video intended to increase my skin care sales, and instead used them to fill me with spirituality. I mean, whatever works, right?

In my search for more of these dynamic women speaking on things like the law of attraction and leveling up, I was divinely led to a woman named

Maru Iabichela. She is the founder of a group and program called Infinite Receiving™.

Hearing her speak online led me to my next important revelations. She reminded me that no one holds the key to your happiness except for you. She said over and over again something that I had never heard before. I kept watching her videos, just to hear her say this. She said, "Your capacity to receive expands infinitely. The universe is ready to give you abundance beyond your wildest imagination - when you are open to receive it."

Those words that really hit me in the heart. Was I open to receive? Was I pushing away all of the things I said I wanted? How was I doing that without even knowing it?

I was certainly open to what was not working, but how open was I to the solutions? The truth was, that I had closed many parts of myself off to the world. It felt as if my soul was out of order. I was now getting more clear that closing myself off - energetically, emotionally, spiritually and physically - was actually causing all of my problems.

Eureka! It felt like she saw straight inside of my soul. I had been turned off and tuned out for a long time. I was realizing that this was the epitome of unconscious living. I was so disconnected and removed from the deepest parts of myself that I woke up one day and felt like a stranger in my own life. I had been on autopilot for a long time. I wasn't going to be able to keep living that way.

This might sound weird, but realizing that I had been living in a disconnected way actually felt like such a huge relief. Now I was beginning to understand what had caused everything to go wrong in my life. I had not been listening to myself.

Now that I knew what was happening, I was finally starting to feel like I had some control. I needed to take back the reins I had given to everyone else. It was time to guide the next chapter of my life exactly where I wanted it to go. I could no longer blame everyone else for my lack of good choices. This internal shift would require awareness, strength, poise and a lot of self-love and compassion. Was I ready for that?

Facing Your Truth
– it will set you free –

I was starting to wake up in my own life. I was starting to see things from a different perspective. It felt amazing. Now, it was time to really take things to the next level. I was getting just enough information to keep me seeking, but I knew that there was something coming. Some bigger changes were on the way. I just wasn't sure in what form they would come in. My intuition was returning and I could feel the change deep in my bones.

Not long after I became intrigued, and a bit obsessive about online coaches and leaders, I made one of the craziest, and best decisions of my life. I was in Colorado visiting my in-laws when I came across one of the many insightful and inspiring Facebook videos of Maru. She was advertising tickets to her live Infinite Receiving™ event in Fort Worth, TX a couple of months away.

It was like an alarm went off. I literally felt a buzzing in my head and a ringing in my ear. I went clicking through her Facebook page to find out more about the event. It was like she wrote the information directly for me. This woman was helping me piece myself back together across time and space. Yet, we had never even met! She was magical. I was actually starting to feel better. I knew I needed to be there. And for the first time in a while I was seeing possibility and positivity.

My soul knew it needed to be at this event to heal, but immediately, my mind started creating problems and feeling the weight of responsibility. My "grown-up" mind was starting to take over the dream of the little excited girl inside of me.

There were some realities present that I hadn't considered that were now becoming clear. Up until that point I had never left my kids for more than a few hours. I really did not have child care for extended amounts of time. I also knew that we weren't in a wonderful financial position at the time. The idea of a trip like that seemed out of the question.

Although these very real problems were bobbing around in my thoughts, I had a moment of clear knowing. I stared at my phone screen, with my thumb hovering over the Buy Now button. I understood in that instant that it was time for me to show up for myself in a big way in order to experience a big change. No one could do this. Not my husband. Not my mom. Not my kids. I had to go. This decision did not require permission. It was going to require certainty, bravery, and blind trust.

At that moment, I did the most illogical thing I had ever done in my life. I ran upstairs and locked myself in the guest bedroom of my in-laws house and logged back into the Infinite Receiving sales page on my phone. I went through the registration process filling out my name, address, and all of the basic information. As I scrolled down to the part that asked for my credit card number my heart began to race and I could feel my face get flush.

Was I really going through with this? I had never spent hundreds of dollars without discussing it with my husband and I had never made an impetuous decision without any logistics figured out. I finished entering my information and nervously pressed the almighty submit button and secretly bought tickets to the event, followed by a round trip plane ticket to Dallas! In a matter of 15 minutes it was done. Non-refundable. Irreversible.

This was my very first brave act of courage and independence and it felt amazing (for a little while). I was showing myself that I meant business about my own happiness becoming a priority. I had just made a huge decision without permission from anyone. A decision that benefitted my needs and wants, and no one else's. I gave myself permission to seize the moment. I had just made a huge step forward in claiming my life back. I was reeling a bit with the energetic rush of my choice. It also felt weird that something so big had just happened in such a short time, and in near silence. I sat for a moment, taking it in.

I took a deep breath and went downstairs to present the news to my family. With each step I took, shame and guilt were beginning to be replaced with excitement and vitality. I ran downstairs, stood right in front of my husband, took another deep breath, put a smile on my face and waited.

He looked up at me and waited for words to come out of my mouth. My voice cracked as I spoke through my fear, "I need to tell you something that I am really nervous about telling you." I felt like I was either going to cry or pass out from being so vulnerable.

The old me would be scared of owning this moment and speak apologetically. But the badass me of this moment would no-way-in-hell stand there like a scared schoolgirl and beg forgiveness. I forced myself to keep going.

"At the end of January I am going to Dallas for a motivational event. I have already purchased the tickets to the event and airline tickets all of which are non-refundable. I am not looking for your permission. I just want you to know that I need this. We need this." I was aware enough to realize that what I said came out of me as one run-on sentence.

I waited for a reply. Although I thought I was acting very stoic, my knees were shaking and I could feel my lips start to quiver. I was actually surprised at the reaction my body was having.

He stood up and took his own deep breath and said, "I don't know exactly what you are doing or what this all means, but you seem truly excited and happy and that is a good start." I'm not sure what I expected, but I was so shocked by his response that I couldn't speak. And for me, that's saying something.

As soon as I said what I needed, he responded - with love. I was making my presence known and he was seeing me stand proud in my power. I was starting to feel hopeful not only about the future of my marriage but the future of my life.

Claim Your Life
– easier said than done –

I'm going to pause here before I continue with my story. Have you ever taken a stand for yourself? Have you started to stake claim to your own life? If you have, you'll know what happens next.

Sure, I had made big steps, but old habits die hard. Underneath the bliss of my selfish decision was an enormous amount of shame and guilt. If you haven't made a selfish choice yet, know that what happens next in my story is completely natural. If you aren't used to standing up for yourself, it will feel bad at first. You'll feel guilty. Don't let that stop you. It is so important to move through those feelings and keep going.

Now, back to my story.

What in the hell was I thinking? Did I literally just spend over $500 of our Christmas money on myself? I was beginning to think that hiring a therapist may have been a healthier way to spend the money. I mean, was I crazy? Was I now chasing

65

inspirational and motivational leaders around the country in order to feel better about myself? Do sane mothers and wives do these kinds of crazy things? Probably not!

Now I found myself soaking in an overflowing tub of shame and guilt. I knew these feelings all too well. I was feeling the aches of worry and fear that I would possibly be taking the slightest moment of time or money away from my family. But now I had gone through with it and there was no turning back. What I needed to do was put on my big girl panties and own this shit like the badass I was returning to.

In my moment of unbridled spontaneity, I finally got it. I realized how good it felt to do something for the good of my own soul. I realized how important it is to take responsibility for your happiness, unleash your power and head towards the things that light you up.

I used to carry such tremendous resentment against my husband because time and time again he would talk about things he had done or experiences he had while on location for work. He would never miss an opportunity that presented itself for him to see or do something new and exciting and to make the most of his time away. Why didn't he feel the guilt I felt? How could he so easily make himself happy without the consideration of others? Most importantly, why was I so incapable of doing the same?

In this moment, the feelings of resentment were beginning to shift into feelings of empathy. I felt like he and I now had something in common. That felt really good in my heart. I realized that maybe, this whole time my husband had been on to something. It felt exhilarating.

If anyone would have asked, there is no way I could have explained or logically justified why I needed to go on this trip. It may have looked like it from the outside, but it didn't feel like I was running away. It felt like I was running towards something important. I was running into a lifeboat that I was certain would take me safely to shore and protect me from the strongest undertow of my life. I needed to feel excited and inspired. I was longing for the feeling of bliss and a break from the monotony that my routines had become. I was feeling butterflies in my stomach and for the first time in a while I was feeling a surge of hope and optimism that I had really missed. It was nice to have that relationship back with joy.

Write Your Reboot
– journal about your spin –

- What has your lowest point (s) looked like so far?

- Where are you right now in your life? What is working and what isn't?

- Would you be okay if nothing changed?

- What are you really scared of?

- What have you given up on? Was it by choice, or necessity? Are you sure?

- When did you last push the boundaries of your comfort zone?

- Where do you see love in your life now?

- Where might you be able to take a situation where you feel like a victim, and shift into a co-creator to change the situation?

- Sitting in discomfort is part of healing. Where are you uncomfortable in your life?

Turn It Off & Wait

Turn It Off & Wait

Taking the time to consciously turn off your spinning mind is certainly not easy. But, really, this is where the magic starts to happen. There are few things more important than an intentional pause. You are likely more clear about what is not working in your life and why. It might be counterintuitive, but it is not quite the time to take action. This is the time to slow down and look inward. Make updates to the system: reflect, pivot your perspective, shift your beliefs and set clear intentions so that you may reboot your life.

A pause is not synonymous with passivity. Pausing is not a weakness. Internal work is the key here, not external work. This is your time to dream. Dream bigger than you ever have before.

Turning Off For The First Time
– this may not feel good at first –

I did it. One month later I had figured out the logistics and was on the first solo trip since motherhood on the way to Dallas, Texas. I was sitting at the airport excited about my first time alone since my two children were born. I sat alone at an airport bar and ordered a glass of wine. This was something I hadn't done since my heyday in the movie business.

There was this welling of immense emotion filling up inside of me that made me feel as if I might explode. Part of me was scared shitless. Part of me was sad that I was going to be away from my kids for 3 days. A whole other part of me was completely elated at the adventure on which I was embarking. It felt confusing, to say the least. I was traveling alone to an event with no one I knew, without my kids. I was going to stay with a roommate I had never met. In all of the unknown, lived a feeling of deep knowing that I was exactly where the Universe wanted me to be at that moment.

I felt a deep urge to share my new awareness with the world! I wanted to go live on social media and tell the world about my first day of being "found." But, my confidence was still hiding in the shadows. My nerves and excitement grew as I heard the overhead announcement to begin boarding the plane.

Here I go. I boarded the plane and settled in my seat. I barely listened to the boarding safety announcements droning over the intercom. "*If you are traveling with a child or someone who requires assistance, secure your mask first, then assist the other person.*" I once again rolled my eyes and pondered the absurdity of asking parents to secure their own oxygen masks before that of their children. What a ridiculous concept. Would any mother actually have it in her to breathe in gulps of air while they watched their child struggle to catch their breath? Doubtful. Who did these airlines think they were kidding with their rules and advice?

Then, for some reason, this announcement I've heard countless times hit me like a ton of bricks. I finally understood what this meant. The logic of this life-saving theory became crystal clear sitting in aisle 13, seat C of this plane to freedom. How can I save my family, if I can't breathe? It was like a bell rang inside my mind.

Then the realization went straight to my heart. I was putting my oxygen mask on first right now so that I could be there to assist those I love. The awareness kept washing over me. If I am not happy and fulfilled, then there is no way for me to have anything of value to offer those I love. The realization kept moving deeper. I realized that the most selfish thing I could do for the people I loved was to forget to care for myself. Because then there would be no oxygen, no love, no support, no compassion left to share with them. If I didn't save myself first, I wouldn't actually be able to help anyone else.

That was the reason I was feeling lost and empty. That was the reason I had not made time, or room in my life for myself, or my own happiness. Because of that, everyone I loved was paying a price. Just the understanding of it made me feel elated! I could see what was happening with so much clarity.

It felt like a sign from the universe that I was heading in the right direction. I felt so connected and alive. Then, I realized the plane was on the tarmac and we were about to take off. Just about the time the wheels on the plane went into motion, the ride of a lifetime began to feel like a death sentence.

As the plane began to rush forward and prepare for take off, I went from having a profound realization about my life to having one of the worst panic attacks of my life. My ego was desperately trying to keep me safe from flying into the unknown. My teeth began chattering so hard that you could hear them crack together. My hands were shaking uncontrollably. I think it appeared as if I was having some sort of seizure. The moment the plane floated into the air, I seriously thought about asking the flight attendant if it was too late for me to get off. My eyes filled with tears.

I began to think that this was my punishment for making such a crazy choice. Obviously I should be home cuddling my babies to sleep! Not on some airplane flying to an event with complete strangers.

By the grace of the heavens, a woman sitting next to me realized that I was not ok. Maybe the bottle of water jerking uncontrollably in my hand gave it away. She was kind enough to begin a conversation with me even though I was clearly in panic. She asked me a very obvious question, "Is this your first time flying?" Little did she know that this was probably my 500th flight. My nerves must have made me look like a newbie. She then asked a more general question, "Are you traveling for business or pleasure?" I immediately began to sob. She said that she was so sorry to bother me and be nosy.

I composed myself, caught my breath and blurted out in one continuous sentence, "I am going to an event called Infinite Receiving because I am ready to receive me back into my life." Can you say awkward? At this point she should have assumed that she had unfortunately been seated next to a batshit crazy woman and asked for a seat change. But she stayed and continued talking to the lunatic...me!

In that magical moment of exclaiming what I was doing out loud, I felt my nervous system gently slow down. It was like the honesty of my proclamation had pressed the reset button. My shakes slowly but surely came to a stop and an overwhelming sense of joy and laughter came pouring out of me.

We proceeded to talk and I began the first honest conversation about what led me to this moment. I shared with her how I was feeling lost and this flight was an attempt to find my self-love again. I told her about my loss of identity and purpose and she listened with intent and compassion. To my surprise, tears began to stream down her face. She told me about her feelings of loss and her admiration for the journey I was on. She told me that my story of bravery was a motivation for her to be more present in her own life and make her happiness as important as those of others.

What just happened? Did my breakdown just help her? I looked out the window and saw the expanse of white fluffy clouds as far as the eye could see. Then I had a beautiful whisper of clarity come flooding in from the Universe. I realized that when we are down below the storm clouds the world can look dark and gloomy. But, if we could take a different perspective and look down from high above the storm we would see that it is only a small portion of the sky that is dark. The rest is full of sun and white clouds that are just around the corner. But we need to survive the storm to see it from this place.

I knew at that moment that I better buckle up for the ride of a lifetime.

I Deserve To Matter
– I value my presence –

With the new realization that I matter swimming around in my mind, courtesy of my flight attendant, I was starting to catalogue the events of my life. What I was seeing wasn't pretty.

First, I had been putting myself last almost every-damn-where in my own life. I was the guest star in my own movie. I was most certainly running my life on the automatic pilot of everyone else's needs. There was no area of my life where I felt truly satisfied. No area of my life felt like it was getting enough of my own attention and affection.

As a result, I felt disconnected from my life. I most certainly felt disconnected from the Universe and God. I felt disconnected from the people that I love. And most of all, I felt disconnected from the ME that I loved so much. The me that I had left behind and forgotten.

What I had not yet admitted to myself is that when you put yourself last, it is usually because you do not love yourself enough to matter to you. I had put the blame on others to avoid taking a long, honest look at myself in the mirror. I felt justified in ignoring my essence because after all, I was doing all the things I was supposed to be doing.

I was a mother and therefore I should give everything to my children. I was the wife of a man who had a career in the movie business. He was passionate about his work and very good at it. Here again, I put his needs ahead of my own, and made it my job to hold down the fort while he lived his passion.

For the record, my husband didn't ask me to do that. He never sat me down and informed me that his needs should rank above mine. I took that on myself. I did that. Even if it meant that I was lonely, and overwhelmed, "a good wife should support her husband." Of course that's what we do for one another. Except for the fact that I was doing it for him and not myself.

The second realization I had while sipping my chardonnay on the plane, in a much more relaxed state, was the awareness of my beliefs. Where did this belief of putting everyone else first actually originate? How did it actually start? Like I said earlier, when I was younger, I was on fire! I put myself and my dreams first. Where did that go? How did I lose it?

The truth is I learned about sacrifice in the name of love from my parents. They told me about it all of the time. I had grown up completely saturated in love from my mother and father. They were amazing. However, I was also constantly reminded of the dreams that both of them had given up in the name of me.

I learned how to be the most loving and supportive parent in the world while at the same time believing the lesson that our dreams have to take a back seat to the happiness of our loved ones. As their child, my needs always took priority over their own because love means sacrifice.

I brought those lessons right into my parenting when I became a proud mother. Of course I believe in family first, but isn't a mother a part of the family? Can't we need the same care and nurturing that we so willingly give to our loved ones?

So with 24 hours in a day, a dad that was suffering

from severe health issues, a traveling husband, dynamic and adventurous kids with many after-school sports and activities, a full-time job, and friends and family to love to spend time with, there was truly nothing leftover just for me. If I took precious time away from those I loved, to take care of number one, then what kind of a selfish narcissistic mother would that make me... right? How could I keep all of the balls in the air if I left to spend time or money on myself?

Yep. That's what I thought. For a long time.

The flight attendant burst into my thought process with a wonderful question. "Is there anything else I can get you?"

I smiled at her and asked her to refill my Chardonnay. Her question was perfect. One I hadn't been asking myself. Was there anything I could do for me? I had a deep sense that this weekend would answer that question.

The truth is that my happiness counts too. The best thing I could do for my kids and my family was to go into this adventure and reclaim my smile. I wanted to teach my kids that their dreams can thrive in the presence of those that love them most. Love did not equate to sacrifice the way I had been taught. We make a choice to become mothers and to love these little humans with all of our hearts. But we can also make a choice to love ourselves and stay connected to our deepest desires and dreams. They can absolutely co-exist.

That is exactly what I was doing. I was headed to Dallas to reclaim my magic. It was time to show myself, my husband and my kids that love means to live your life with passion, maximize every day, every moment and every minute of the gift of life.

The Courage To Do It
– scared shitless –

You should know that this was actually the first time in my life that I had gone anywhere all alone. I have been to many places and done many things but never as a party of one. I was not a person who enjoyed the solitude of doing things by herself. Dinner, movies, trips. I believed all of them required accompaniment. Yet here I was, checking into a hotel to get a room key for a room that I was going to share with someone I had never met before. Two years ago... shit, two months ago, you would have never caught me doing this. Now I saw it as my lifeline.

My nerves were firing through the roof. Every step I took towards that hotel room gave me the desperate urge to flag down a taxi and be taken right back to the airport where I could fly home to the safety of my home and kids and the place I had left my sane mind. Instead, I forced myself to walk to my room. I forced myself to stay present and breathe into each moment. Each second was spent pushing thoughts of doubt and fear aside to allow room for hope and possibility to enter.

This was not crazy.

This was not crazy.

This was not crazy.

Listening to myself repeat these words made me sad. I was so worked up! Simply by walking to a hotel room for a weekend retreat. Had I grown so accustomed to fearful thoughts that it became my default setting? It certainly seemed that way.

I finally made it to the 6th floor. Things seemed a bit in slow motion. I raised my hand with the key card in it, put it in the electronic lock, and opened the door.

Inside, was a very lovely woman named Laura. She happened to be about my age. We hit it off immediately. Within 5 minutes we knew that we were both mothers of 2 children. We were both in marriages with an uncertain fate. And unfortunately, we both were in the middle of a deep crisis of identity. It was like kismet.

Here we were in Dallas for the same exact reasons. We both felt lost. We both came to this event needing to find the parts of our soul that we had left behind somewhere in our twenties. We both needed to connect back with the energy and passion of our younger selves to continue on the next part of our life's adventure.

We both bonded about the guilt of feeling so alone and stuck in our very full lives with beautiful families and friends. Only perfect strangers, just hours before, this beautiful woman and I had begun to discover we were traveling down the very same path.

I started to relax even further. I was in the perfect place. My whole body knew it. It felt like a divine synchronicity. I took this as my little wink from my angels. They were telling me that I was exactly where I was supposed to be. I knew that I had arrived somewhere that would change my life forever. I could feel it in my bones.

Now it was about so much more than just lighting myself up. I wanted to become the equivalent of a thousand ornate lanterns rising up into the vastness of the Universe to light up the freaking galaxy. I just wasn't quite sure how it would happen. Have you ever been in a place or situation that you felt would change your life but you were not sure how? It has a particular feeling, doesn't it?

I was feeling my fear and moving through it again, and again, and again. Because I was moving through this fear instead of letting it stop me (which was my old habit) I was now creating some momentum and movement in my life. I could feel it.

Please know, it is so very okay to feel fear. It is a normal reaction in your body. The key here is to acknowledge it and to continue. If you let your fear stop you, you'll stay right. where. you. are.

The Journey Of Self-Discovery Begins
– hold on! –

As our very first day of the event unfolded, I was provided with an abundant amount of evidence to prove that I was exactly where I was supposed to be. Coming here had been the right decision. First of all, I was on a mission to make this weekend mean something that was going to make the "sacrifice" worth it. Somehow I had no choice but to return from this event changed or risk facing the humiliation of making all these crazy decisions without a payoff. That energy kept the realizations coming.

I had a monumental epiphany as I was preparing for the first event of the day. No one here knew me. No one knew any version of me except for the one they were going to meet today. They had no previous point of reference to compare me to. On this day I had a clean slate and I was free of judgments of myself. This realization felt great!

When I entered the first event of the day, I saw a beautiful and powerful woman standing on stage emceeing the event. At that moment, my intuition and clairvoyance returned. I knew that an important bond was going to be developed with this current stranger and myself. I knew very clearly that this woman would be an important part of my life. I had no idea who she was, but I knew she would be my friend.

As the day continued, so did the magic. One of the speakers of the day was a lady on stage doing an Akashic record meditation. "A what?" you ask. That is exactly the question I was asking myself. She had just finished discussing timelines and the basics on how the Akashic records work. The whole concept was new to me. I had never even heard of the word before. But, as I listened, I began to feel this deep connection to the content that she was pouring out to us. The ideas seemed radical and yet felt so organic.

If I was understanding her correctly, she was explaining that deja vu's exist because time is not linear. We can travel backwards and forwards through our timeline whenever we want. Basically what that means is that our present self is able to communicate with our past and future self. How cool is that?

As the woman on stage led us into an amazing meditation, she asked us to start controlling our breath. The voice in my head was shouting, "WHAT? But there is no way that's right! Let's try this crazy shit out and see what happens." Almost as if to prove this whole experiment doomed from the start, I followed along with what she told us to do.

As luck would have it, I ended up seated next to the emcee of the event. Her name was Patricia. Yes, the same woman that I knew was going to matter in my life. She and I had the opportunity to get to know each other throughout that day. As it turns out, the feeling of sympatico was mutual. How cool is that?!

So, here I am seated next to her and a woman named Inez during this meditation. We closed our eyes and locked hands with each other as I tried to contain all of the excitement of the day. I took two deep breaths and asked my future self to come back to me in this present moment with a sign that the future was safe and great and it was all going to turn out ok.

What I am going to tell you next will seem like a made up story from a person who was experimenting with plant medicine, or LSD. I can assure you that is not the case. I had my phone sitting on the table directly in front of me during the meditation. When she asked us to open our eyes, I looked down at my phone in utter disbelief. My phone was open to a new note and the words "I Love You" were the only thing written on the note. I had not opened the notes myself and I certainly hadn't typed that. I looked at Patricia and asked her if she wrote that to me. Nope. She did not. Inez had not either. They both thought it was ridiculous of me to ask since our hands had been locked. I began to feel the blood start to rise in my body and my brain start to zoom into overdrive trying to find the logical explanation. I had nothing. I decided that for once I was going to avoid overthinking the situation and allow the flow of the moment and of the people and experiences to lead me.

My normal response to the unknown has been to think of each possible outcome, and each scenario, and to analyze each and every piece of data to make the smartest conclusions. This time, ease and surprise felt right. I was enjoying the freedom and excitement of this lighthearted attitude. Even though magical synchronicities were happening all around me, I was starting to relax. I felt connected to myself wholly. Past, present and future. I believed that my future self was sending me a message of love and reassurance that I was going to be fine. As I quieted my mind, fears, and ego I started to feel the downpour of guidance and messages come through me with abandon.

Each moment afterwards continued to be utterly magical. I felt strongly connected to my intuition and inner guidance throughout the entire day. That alone felt like a miracle. I hadn't felt connected to those parts of myself in a very long time. It was a connection I didn't even realize I had missed.

I had forgotten to live my life with these connections to the less physical parts of myself. I even remembered how good it felt to be led by your heart instead of your mind. It had been so long since I had done this that I forgot this was even something I could do. I remembered the fond feelings of having your body tingle when you act on a desire that was sent to your brain directly from your heart.

It had been so long since an idea had kept me up most of the night. When I was younger, I did this all of the time. It felt as if it had been whispered into my ear straight from God. It felt like a connection that was meant for me and only me. I used to smile when I had trouble writing in my journal because the words were flowing into my mind faster than I could write them on the page. This was an experience that I had missed and was starting to welcome back. I know the difference in how it feels to act from inspiration rather than logic and ego.

The women I met over the course of the next 48 hours were so much like me. Women who had passions, gifts, and talents that they were trying to fit into their lives as wives and mothers. They were working to get the absolute most out of their experience as a woman. They were not merely trying to "get through it." None of these women were willing to sacrifice themselves in order to fulfill their responsibilities to those they loved. Yes! I had landed in the perfect place. I was actually at an event filled with 200 women that believed life doesn't require you to give up on you in order to be there for others. It felt like heaven.

It was not that I had never met a woman like that before. What seemed so magical is that we were all there because we were ready to enter into our next level of womanhood, and own the shit out of our soul's purpose. Honestly, it felt more like an initiation than an event. I was getting more fueled and powered up by the minute. By the end of the first day I had some new friends that saw me for the Linda I was becoming with each breath. For the Linda I was once and almost gave up on. For the upgraded me that now had motherhood and experience to add to her magical potion. I could really feel it. I was starting to like my own company again.

"I get by with a little help from my friends." The Beatles.

You Are The Light
– and always have been –

I woke up that morning feeling a million times changed from the woman I had been only 24 hours before. I felt powerful and magical. I was proud of the assurance that was coursing through my veins. It felt as I had been reinstated back into life and had walked through the portal of the authentic me.

I was feeling excited and ready for Day 2. Within a few hours of getting started, we were given an exercise to partner up with someone. We were partnered up based on answers to some randomly assigned questions. As it turns out, I ended up partnered with Inez. She was one of the women I had locked hands with the day before. We didn't have much time the day before to learn about each other. Now we got it.

Within seconds of getting to know each other, we were laughing. We were both teachers! She had been a school teacher, but had retired and started her own business. She was guiding and teaching women entrepreneurs how to be strong and confident. She also taught them to make serious boss money running companies of their own. What? That was an option for teachers as a next step? You could go from teaching to owning a company, making serious money, and traveling the world getting paid to teach to your passion? I had seriously missed the memo on what was possible!

I sat with her and listened to her speak about her passion and the money she was earning. I began to feel this heat rising inside my chest. Something was brewing. The feeling was intense. I knew something new was headed my way, but I didn't quite know what it represented. Yet.

It had been several years since I had decided that I wanted to evolve from teaching small children. The idea of teaching women to be more empowered seemed like an exciting alternative. But, time and again, before I could even really begin to dream about new possibilities, I would deter myself from the opportunity at each breath.

Each time the idea of a new adventure would emerge, self doubt would creep in about my lack of qualifications. Who was I to stand in front of women and teach anything of value? Me? I couldn't even handle the life that I had without becoming invisible. Who would want to learn from me? Clearly, badassery had skipped me when God was handing out gifts and talents.

After spending almost half an hour with Inez, I continued around the room meeting other women that had their own stories of life conquering quests. I was in a room filled with unbelievable women who seemed to be rockin' motherhood and womanhood. Strangely, time and time again they all shared their feelings of an identity loss like mine. Was this a phenomenon of women in the world? Are we all trying to find our rightful place?

By the time I had made my way around the room, I was exhausted from the range of emotions that had passed through me. From shame to jealousy to sheer awe. I looked each woman in the eye at the end of our interaction and thanked them with deep intensity for the privilege of the connection. Each time, I received a very unexpected answer in return. "Your light is so bright! You feel magical."

Me? Magical? A light? I received about a dozen

variances on that response by the time the day was over. What were they seeing in me that I had been unable to see in myself? What was the worst and scariest thing that could happen to me if I actually allowed myself to believe that they could be right?

Embracing Your Magic
– slowly but surely –

In the middle of this amazing experience, being embraced by all of these women, my mind shot to another place entirely. I went back and reclaimed a piece of my magic. Let me share what happened for me! It was truly...magical.

I have to share something with you. This was the most difficult topic to write about because of my relationship with magic. For a long time, I didn't understand what was happening to me. I'm just now learning to embrace and integrate this side of me as a part of my normal life. Here goes.

Even though I didn't quite understand it, I had spent most of my youth feeling very comfortable with the insight, intuition and messages being received from God, Universe, Source (or whatever name you prefer to give to that higher power and intelligence) that is always there for us. I knew in a way that it made me different and unique. I used to embrace that. I had made some very extreme decisions and had used my power of intuition to guide me to the answers.

For example, I moved to NYC right out of college with barely a dollar to my name. With my cousin's help and love, I had a safe and beautiful place to stay and within weeks I had landed a job in the movie business courtesy of her boyfriend. To everyone else, it seemed like the most insane choice to make but, I knew in my gut that I was making the right decision.

Even though in my current reality, my husband embraced the "witchy" parts of me, there came a point in our marriage when my power became my foe. When my jealousy and insecurity began to take over our relationship, I felt that my instincts were to blame. Where were they now that I needed them the most? How could they abandon me in my greatest hour of need? But what I could not see then was that I had stopped listening even though the messages were still speaking to me.

I convinced myself that my messages, and intuition could not be trusted. In that lack of trust, I made a subconscious choice to shut it all down. But, of course, without my inner truth and guidance I began to spin out of control. I felt powerless in the dim light of awareness that I was not accustomed to without my magic. Choices and decisions became hard to make without my little voice guiding my way.

My intuition remained quiet until that day in Colorado when I spoke clearly to the Universe and declared the return of all that I was. Making the scary decision to go to Dallas all alone was when I began feeling my light start to brighten. Armed with evidence from the people at the event that they could actually see the real me, I knew I was slowly rebuilding my relationship to my magic and intuition. Since then I have used it to create some of the greatest successes and joy of my life - even this book.

It took me going through a lot of pain and discomfort to remember that the expert in my life was actually (drum roll please) ME. I was starting to take back the power I had silenced for so long. I was just starting to get a taste of confidence and self-esteem. What I didn't realize yet is that there was so much more to come.

What I have not talked about yet (so in full and

uncomfortable disclosure here I go) was my untamed ability to channel messages from what I call Source. Through these channeled messages came even more clarity. Allow me to explain.

My dad told me when I was a little girl that I would often tell him not to worry because God was with us, and he was telling me that everything was going to be alright. As I got older, this gift enhanced quite a bit. I was able to receive very precise messages.

In another, bigger example, a colleague of mine shared that she was looking for her estranged father and was not having much luck. Days later, I received a very clear message that her dad was somewhere in Arizona. The message was so crystal clear that it even surprised me. "Tell her to start looking in Arizona." Alrighty then, How, exactly, was I going to tell this woman this information? Did she even believe in this stuff? Would she even believe me?

I sat at my desk for hours trying to figure out a way to get the message to her while also trying not to sound like a crazy person. The more I tried to ignore the message, the louder it got. Until

I finally gave in and shared what I knew. I was sweating in the fear of how she might respond. "Listen, I know this may not make any sense, but try looking for him in Arizona." She replied, "Well, you are right. That makes no sense. He can't be in Arizona. He's from NY and still lives there from the info I have been able to gather." With her rebuttal, I had no way to explain.

I immediately started to shrink. What had I been thinking? All of a sudden, I wished I hadn't said a word, and we could just drop it. Someone walked up and asked her a question. I let it go and hurried away whispering, "Please forget, please forget, please forget!" quietly to myself.

I didn't speak another word of it until the day she came to work balling. She ran up to my desk and gave me a huge hug. "You are not going to believe this. I found him. In Arizona! Exactly where you said." I could not get the thought out of my head that she had actually found her dad in Arizona. That message was real. That message was real. I actually did have gifts. My next thought was that I needed to do something with these gifts. Since then, I have received much more validation that the messages were accurate. This just seemed to add to the *extra* that people always used to describe me. I really did not mind. It was something just for me and I liked it. I knew I had magic.

So now that I was ready to embrace my magic, I wanted to actually make it front and center of my life. If this ability was showing up for me, then it must be for a purpose because that is why God grants them to us. It was becoming clear from my time away that my purpose was IMPACT. I wanted to use this wise sage-like voice deep in my soul to help other women remember their greatness just like Maru had done for me. Watch out world! A magical woman with a mission is bulletproof.

Now back to the event. My consciousness came back to the room. I closed my eyes while in that room full of hundreds of excited women. I focused inward. In a very small whisper in my head, I started apologizing. I apologized for the arrogance that I displayed in shutting down the very voice whose only mistake had been to use me to send messages to people who could not hear them on their own. I apologized for all of the countless times that I had screamed at life, and God, and the Universe for the shit in my life that seemed broken. I had many times begged for solutions to my problems, and then completely ignored the answers. The same answers that I kept screaming to go away. I could feel the tears streaming down my face.

My heart filled with love as I opened my eyes once again to the presence of the incredible people in this room. I immediately felt an overwhelming sense of gratitude for reconnecting with this part of me. I started to feel the bubbly excitement of a little girl. It was like I found that part of myself again, and she was right there with me. That night I went to bed with a heart full of love and gratitude. As I closed my eyes to fall asleep I heard a message loud and clear that said, "Welcome back to your magic. We've missed you." I knew that as I slept that night my internal dialogue was charging and my system was gently upgrading.

This trip was turning out to be the medicine I needed to swallow to heal my heart and soul. Once upon a time, before adulthood had taken over my imagination, I used to innately know that I was a divine being of Source energy. What I had just done that day was step into the chambers of my soul and declared, "I remember you. I know how great you are. Thank you for coming back for me."

Sometimes You Need A Pep Talk
– for you, by you –

Maru had created a tribe of women that were all called in by her message and presence here in Dallas. She had trusted the message that she channeled and used it to help and change the lives of many women around the world. I knew that by reopening the gates to my divine guidance I would be able to follow in her footsteps and start receiving messages that God would transmit to me in an effort to help humanity. I had called her my muse on several occasions and this was starting to play itself out in reality.

On my final night in Texas, I was getting ready to go out to dinner with some of the girls that I had met. As I was getting all dolled up to head out, I looked at myself in the mirror. I could feel the judgemental and cruel self-talk creeping up in my mind as I looked at my reflection in the glass. The words were practically memorized. They could be applied to almost any situation I found myself in. If only I was thinner, then I could dress in an outfit I really loved for dinner. If only I knew how to properly apply make-up then I could make myself look gorgeous. If only I was... and then filled in the blank with all the things I was not but wished to be. But on this evening, I had found my light. There was no way in hell that I was going to let that cruel voice living in my head dim my light, or take it away from me. I looked in the mirror and did one of the weirdest things I have ever done. I stared into my own eyes and had a serious pep talk with myself. It went something like this...

> "Linda, get over yourself. No one is paying attention to your outfit or your make-up. You are beautiful inside and out. You are enough for anyone that you meet. Everyone that goes out with you tonight is going to witness your sparkle and find warmth in your rays! You've got this! You are magic and tonight the world sees it."

And with that I winked at my reflection and continued getting ready for an incredible night. I had come all the way here for experiences and I was not going to miss a single one. I knew what I had to offer and it was time to bring it to the table. Literally, the dinner table.

Write Your Reboot
– journal about turning off &
waiting –

- What worries you the most about building the future of your dreams?

- What are your biggest takeaways so far?

- Does it really matter what others think of you? Why or why not?

- What beliefs do you have around your goals that may stop you from achieving them?

- Do you wait for perfection to take action? What is that keeping you from doing?

- If you could give yourself a pep talk, what would you say?

Turn It Back On & Reboot Your Life

Turn It Back On & Reboot Your Life

You have arrived. Welcome to your reboot. The space where self love exists and resides at the helm. All other decisions and priorities take a back seat to putting your oxygen mask on first. Lead your life with integrity, love and understanding for yourself and others.

It may have been a long journey to arrive at this place of peace, love, and trust. Do not regret any of the steps that have gotten you here as each and every one has built your path to this moment in time.

You may not be sure what the future holds and what adventures await. But what you know now is that if the road is ever bumpy again (and it will be) you can simply turn off, wait, and then reboot.

Updating Your System
– soul-level upgrades –

Welcome back! You have been through a reboot.

So now I had a new dream and a clear purpose to take home. I wanted to gather a group of women that would come together for the common purpose of seeing themselves in alignment with a message that I had channeled and could offer the world. Just hearing myself say that I felt worthy and valuable enough to want to put my message out there was evidence of the shifts the weekend had created within me.

I was ready to step back into my life. On the Sunday morning of our departure, I shared a ride to the airport with four of the most badass women I had ever met. We spoke passionately about how the event had awoken something inside each of us, and how good it felt to feel so alive again. We all laughed when I joked that the world was about to get lit up now that all the dragons have awoken from their slumber.

I was absolutely feeling like a dragon. Strong and powerful and full of fire and light. This time I was not afraid to share that power with the world. Hopefully this feeling would last when I got off the airplane and landed safely home. I'll admit it. I was scared.

What if they didn't want this updated me? I was done with shape shifting in versions of me that would accommodate other people, even my own family. I knew I was returning home as a new and improved version of myself. All I could do was hope and pray that they would embrace me and be open to the new found confidence that I was bringing home with me.

Unless you are Peter Pan, all adventures must at some point come to an end. We never want magical experiences that capture our heart to end. Yet those experiences are the most magical when we integrate what we learned from them back into our regular, everyday lives. This way we don't leave the adventure behind, we take it with us. We show it off to our family and friends. We bring it home like our favorite souvenir and share with everyone the memories that are evoked. This was my plan for coming home. I wanted everyone to know what had happened, and how I felt so different.

On the plane ride back, I reflected on the three short days that had rocket launched me into years of personal development. I giggled to myself as I calmly and confidently sat in my airplane seat with very little leg room, listening to the woman give the oxygen mask talk. I smiled to myself at the new meaning held inside the message.

Before long, I was sipping on red wine, and remembering that just days ago on a flight going in the opposite direction, I had one of the worst panic attacks of my entire life. I remembered with love and forgiveness, the panic that had made me want to turn around, jump off a plane in mid-air, and skip the entire event to get back home to safety. I beamed with pride at the woman who was returning with assurance and self-love.

Although it felt like an instant transformation, deep down I knew that this had been brewing in my soul for years. About halfway into the flight, the man sitting next to me woke from his nap and struck up a conversation with me. We talked for a while about his job and family and then he asked me what I did. I replied that I was an elementary school teacher and an aspiring writer, creator, and thought leader. He smiled at me and said, "Seems like that would be no problem for a woman like yourself. It's possible." I thanked him for seeing me and giving me the evidence I needed. Once again, I shed inflight tears, but this time they were coming from a place of gratitude and contentment.

Clearly things were actually starting to shift. The moment I heard his validation, I knew that my invisibility cloak had been shed. I was showing up for the world to see. This was my first sighting of my new self. There would be many more that would come from this magical weekend of awakening.

I kept on beaming. I sat back in my window seat and stared at the white puffy clouds and bright sun. This is what it is like to be flying above the storm. It is always clear when you get high enough. As the sun's warmth beamed through the small window of the aircraft I closed my eyes and made a silent prayer that the people I love most in the world waiting for me down below would know that my absence was a brave display of love.

As I stepped off the plane my heart was beating out of my chest and my mouth was parched. I felt like a new woman on the inside but how would I get that across on the outside? I was greeted by my two beautiful and adoring children that I had missed more than life itself. I was terrified that they would resent me for my absence but by the intensity of their hugs I could tell that they felt nothing but love. My kids asked over and over again, "Mommy how was your trip?" and I replied with, "Amazing. I am so happy and I cannot wait to tell you all about it." I had been missed and my arrival home was off to a good start. It would be another week before my husband came home from location to visit. This was going to be the true test of whether these mindset and spiritual changes I had made were going to be carried into my daily life.

One week later my kids and I were at the airport anxiously awaiting my husband to arrive. As we stood at the gate, I gave myself yet another much needed pep talk. This time I was not going to do what I normally do because then I would ensure the results that I normally get. Usually I wait for him to make the first move, and I am screaming within minutes for his lack of urgency in wanting me.

As I watched him walk out of the gate, I decided to take the reins and take control. I nervously walked and gave him a tender and passionate kiss while holding his face and said, "Thanks for giving me time to get away. Things are going to be very different." He kissed me back as tenderly and replied "You look happy. I like that."

That is when the wheels started to spin in my mind. Could it be that my unhappiness was the culprit for all the pain and suffering in my marriage? Is it possible that I blamed him for the misery inside of my own heart? The answers would take a while to figure out but in the meantime I was excited for a second chance at happiness.

For that weekend my husband was home, things were not miraculously fixed. But, the change in energy was certainly palpable. There was less of a fear deep in my heart that I would be left alone and unloved. I figured that if that was how this story ended, then I would be able to figure it out. But what I would not settle for is the desperate attempts to be loved and desired. Nothing had changed physically about me and yet there was a distinct change in the way I carried myself and the way that he responded. I had proved to myself while in Texas that people would see me the way that I saw myself and that changed everything.

The next morning was Saturday. In the past, I would not have left the kids alone with my husband to do something only for me. This day was totally different. I woke up and kissed all three of them on the forehead and told my husband that I would be back around noon. They could enjoy each other's company until I returned. I could see the surprise in his eyes when he asked where I was going and I proudly responded with a visit to the spa. I can promise you he was not expecting that! He told me to have a good time and off I went.

As I drove my car to the salon, I waited for the guilt and shame to set in. I waited for the phone call from my husband asking me to stop being selfish and get my ass home. And I waited and waited. And nothing. Neither scenario played out. However, there was something far more unexpected in its place: excitement and gratitude. While sitting comfortably in the massage chair while getting pampered with a pedicure and feeling amazing, I received a text from my husband that simply read, "I love you."

My second weekend home I began to feel safe enough to have friends over and continue the process of reintegration. Deep down I was curious to see how my friends would accept me or would they even notice a difference. A few of my best friends came to my house to have wine and cheese and hear stories about my adventure away. My best friend Lisa was the first to arrive and within minutes of being at my house she said, "I see it." I said, "what do you see?" Her reply made me cry and laugh at the same time. There was a sense of both surprise and relief at her response. "You. I see you." My eyes flooded with more tears and we hugged and I knew that I already had a tribe of my own. I felt connected to my life in a way that I had not felt in a long while. This was the beginning of turning my power back on and trying to reboot my life from the mess that I had created.

It's Just A Phase
– always –

I was quite a big tomboy growing up. No matter how hard my mom tried she couldn't get me to wear dresses. She begged and pleaded for me to dress in something other than jeans and t-shirts but that was what I loved the most. Her friends and family would tell her not to worry because it was "just a phase." Later in my teens, I started to like boys and put posters up on my wall of guys like Bon Jovi and Rob Lowe because I thought they were so hot. My mom told my dad not to spend too much time worrying about it because, "It was just a phase."

I went from one relationship to another in my twenties because I found it really difficult to commit to one person. I was told that it too was, "just a phase." that I would outgrow. Then at 44 years old I had one of the greatest epiphanies of my life. I was shopping for journals with my daughter and came across one that read, "It's Just a Phase" with a picture of the moon on the cover.

OMG! Guess what people?? My mom was right. (Don't tell her I said so!) Every moment of every day of our entire lives is part of a phase. We are constantly shifting in and out of phases of alignment. In each moment we are experiencing a phase. Every moment of what we experience is meant to grow and expand us to the next phase or level. Just like a video game. The whole point of playing the game at each level is to qualify for the next and so on.

When coming back from Dallas I heard that same phrase mentioned about me again. A lot of my friends and family called my new smiles and giggles, "a phase that I was going through." I heard, "she just got home from a weekend without the kids. It's a phase. She'll be back to herself in a few days." Hearing that felt disheartening. They couldn't yet see what I felt. They didn't have the magical experiences and awakenings I had gone through. I also noticed that they didn't have the clarity or the light I had found.

So, what did this current phase look like? Since coming home, one of the biggest changes I made was to my routine. I knew I had to form new habits for my mind, body, and soul. Ones that helped me to see, remember and hold my own light. I was afraid that if I allowed the same energy loop to play in my mind, and let those sabotaging behaviors in just a little, they would end up like pesky house guests, and try to overstay their welcome. I didn't want to go back to being engulfed in my pain. Each day I woke up and spent a few moments envisioning the new person that I was becoming.

Yes I was in a phase. I'm now happily in my fourth year of this phase of myself. I proudly reclaim the me I have always wanted to be. I honor this phase, and how much better, more aligned and clear I feel. It is my hope and prayer that the next phase of my life is even more of an evolution forward. Into what yet, I can't imagine. But, I'm pretty certain that I couldn't have imagined this phase sitting in my previous cocoon. I hope that I get even closer to my magic so that I can support others seeking their own. I can't wait to see my next phase. I'm sure it will be glorious.

Change The Way You Feel About You

– and everything changes –

I had not seen or loved myself in years. That much was now painfully clear. I don't really know if I knew what self-love meant. Obviously I thought I loved myself. But, did I really? Do you really? I mean sure, I had looked in the mirror and saw my face and hair to get ready for work. But I had not been looking deeper. I wasn't taking a look at how I felt about myself. I had failed to look inside to see how I felt about many things in my life. Or even to know that I could.

What I had been doing instead of looking at how I felt, was to look at how others felt about me. I had been working under the assumption that *that* was where I would find the love for myself. Who knew it had to come from me first? I certainly didn't. Instead, I sought it every time I looked into the eyes of those I loved most: my husband, mother, children, friends. Instead of finding the love I needed, it felt like all I saw was disappointment and judgement.

I believed that if I adjusted what they saw in me that look of disappointment would leave them. I just knew that if I changed who I was they would look at me with the love and compassion I needed. Then I would feel better about myself. But that was no longer working. That belief was turning my life inside out.

Because of my recent life-altering experience, I now knew that they were just reflecting back to me how I felt about myself. It wasn't their disappointment they were showing me, it was my own. Ouch.

Here's how I know what I'm saying is true. The moment that I changed the way I felt about myself on the inside was the exact moment that I noticed the change in how my loved ones reacted to me. When I stood up for myself, and made the crazy decision to go to Dallas, my husband was there for me and agreed. I did not expect that. When I started to do things that interested me, he became interested in me and what I was up to. We even started dating again! When I started seeing me, he responded.

When I started to make how I felt important, I realized that I needed some routines to support me. I wasn't used to self-love. So, I was going to have to make sure that it was a part of each day. I would love to tell you that it was easy, but self-love didn't come easily or naturally to me. It felt awkward and clunky. I realized that I was going to have to give it a little nudge to come to life.

At first it began with positive affirmations wherever my eyes could possibly land. I used sticky notes, lipstick, and pretty much anything I had on hand to write affirmations on every mirror in my house. I wrote them on my hands with a pen and on my vision boards with markers until I could see the words in my mind even with my eyes closed. I began to turn these chores into routines until they had become a habit.

I made sure that my daughter watched my process unfold. I didn't want her to have to wait until she was a full-grown woman to learn the act of self-love. I wanted to emulate for her the bravery that it takes to stand in your power and renew a failing part of your life - at any stage. I wanted to teach through example. I wanted to make her proud that her mom was a risk-taker, and not taking one day of life for granted any longer. I wanted her to understand how it could be different for her than it was for me. In my 40's, I was actually having to teach myself to fall in love with the real and authentic me again. How could I have allowed myself to lose the love for me? I felt so in love with myself and life when I was younger.

As with all new endeavors, little by little, the love I was giving to myself, began to permeate the hearts of those I loved. Unlike before, I was being showered with love and compliments and encouragement that I had not received in quite a while. Even from my husband. What was more and more clear was that the lack of positivity had been coming from me all along. Oh man. That was a hard pill to swallow. As soon as I owned my confidence and self-esteem things around me seemed to shift. People close to me began to treat me differently. They had probably been seeing it all along. I just was not open enough to receive their love. They would tell me I was glowing and that I looked beautiful. Now I actually believed them.

Moving Out Of Fear
– and into action –

My lowest point in the backyard of my house, was not one that I am proud of. I would not wish that experience on my worst enemy. However, like all rainbows, they usually show up after a nice big storm. My lowest point forced me into an awareness that created an empty space for me to step into my power. That was my rainbow after my backyard storm. I was given the ability to recreate my reality into the magic that is still unfolding today.

My light was finding its purpose on this planet. I had wanted to write a book my entire life. Each time I would sit at the computer to scribe, my excuses were stronger than my will. I let my fear stop me. Each and every time. In each moment, I now knew that I had the ability to choose love or fear. I had been feeding fear for a while.

Long ago I had read the story of the Cherokee legend that many of you may already be familiar with. This is the Story of Two Wolves. It is completely relevant to where I was in the process of writing my book.

The story starts out between a Cherokee grandfather and grandson. The elder caught the boy arguing with some other boys, and had stopped the commotion. "A fight is going on inside me," he said to the boy. "It is a terrible fight and it is between two wolves. One wolf is evil – he is anger, envy, sorrow, regret, greed, arrogance, self-pity, guilt, resentment, inferiority, lies, false pride, superiority, and ego." He continued, "The other wolf is good – he is joy, peace, love, hope, serenity, humility, kindness, benevolence, empathy, generosity, truth, compassion, and faith. The same fight is going on inside you – and inside every other person, too."

The grandson thought about it for a minute. He then asked his grandfather, "Which wolf will win?" The Cherokee elder simply replied, "The one you feed."

That had been my story for almost a decade. I had been feeding the fear and the doubt that were keeping me locked inside of a cage. A cage to which I held the key to unlock anytime I wished. I had been living inside the confines of my fear, and I wanted out. Until the day that I decided to feed the other wolf. That day I made peace with my mistakes. I used that as the fuel to head in the direction of my potential. It was time to start writing.

Many of us are told from a very young age what the acceptable parameters are for living our lives. That's the cage we're put in. We are told where our barriers begin and end. It is very clear that there are labels and judgments for those who venture outside those barriers.

Who was I to write a book? I'm an elementary school teacher, shouldn't I just stay in my lane? Who would want to hear my story? I had been listening to terrible thoughts like these that my mind had been feeding me. It was past-time to rebel against these doubts in my mind.

Then one day, I was walking around Home Goods trying to find furniture to spruce up my home and get inspired. My phone alarm went off and as I looked down I saw my daily motivational quote pop across the screen that read, "the only things you fail at are the things you do not try." As soon as I saw it I knew the Universe was speaking to me. If I did not write this book then I was already failing. The worst was already happening.

I rushed out of the store with my heart racing through my chest. There was not a second to waste. I nervously dialed the numbers to the editor that was recommended to me, Misti Patrella. We got on a call and as they say... the rest is history.

I am clearly writing this book. I am going to ensure the right people read it even if that feels scary. Point in fact, you are reading it right now. That's one win. Second win, I busted out of my book cage.

Cracking The Cocoon
– it's time to emerge –

I introduced you to my dear friend Tony, and what he meant to me in the beginning of this book. Shoot, he even helped me title it. But, there are other things you should know. He had dreams that he kept on the side waiting for the right time to live them out. Unfortunately, his time here on Earth was far shorter than he had planned for, and those dreams were laid to rest by his side.

As I walked into his hospital room to visit him for what would be the last time, I saw my 47 year old best friend fading more and more. I grieved for the dreams that he would never get to experience. He lived a very full life and touched more hearts than can ever be counted. I only wish that he had been granted the time to fulfill all of his wishes and desires.

During his funeral I had a realization. I vowed, sitting there in a room full of tears and loss to take away the lessons that his time on Earth had taught me. It was clear to me that dreams were meant to be lived. They are not just movies that are meant to entertain your mind while you sleep.

Dreams and passions are meant to be manifested and experienced in this lifetime. That is why we are here. I wished Tony had been around to give me the advice as the older brother that he always felt like. He would have looked at me with a sideways smile and told me the words that would have made it all better. He would have asked, "Linda, have you tried to reboot? You know it's time." We both would have laughed, and my smile would have returned.

Now that he is gone, I feel like he has passed the torch to me. It's my job now, knowing he couldn't, to go after all of my dreams. If I want to truly live out my service to the world then I need to tap into my dreams and passions and use those to show me my next moves.

Your soul knows what you came into this life to be and do. All it needs is trust on our part to follow it wherever it leads. I spent far too long not taking any action for fear that I was not good enough. These last few years have shown me that I am good enough for my dreams. They are mine because they are meant for me. All I have to do is be brave in my desire to follow the calling of my heart.

If I wanted to help people change their lives, it meant that I needed to change my own. I needed to figure out what made me feel so fulfilled and inspired that my fear around taking the next steps would just go away. Time to figure out what that was.

Without real clarity on how to integrate my learnings into my next career, I went back to my teaching career, a happier version of myself. Things were great for a while, but there was now a change in my perception. I truly enjoyed teaching for a decade, but I could feel more than ever the calling to move to the next phase of my evolution.

I didn't know what I wanted to do next, I just knew it was time to make a change. This career didn't quite fit anymore. It's my guess that a caterpillar feels the same way right before it becomes a butterfly. That cocoon must start to feel uncomfortable and constrictive before it emerges as its new self.

I could feel the cocoon around me shifting. As a matter of fact, I came home from school after the first day back at work, and stayed up long after I had put my kids to bed. I had these surges of energy that kept pushing sleep away. I took out my journal and wrote the following:

Cocoon to Butterfly: The Ponderings of a Caterpillar at the Moment of Transformation

My skin is so tight and I can feel the cracks start to form. At first there are just a few so I try to run to the rescue of each one with the best patch I have available. I have an uncontrollable desire to stretch, and yet I know with certainty that this will cause these cracks to grow larger until inevitably I will be separated from my cocoon. There is a part of me that is excited by the unknown possibilities of what will happen to me once this shell that I have been carrying around is shed.

Even though I have a knowing that it will feel light and free and allow me to possibly fly, I have had this cocoon for so long. I don't know life without it. It has been there for me through thick and thin. I wonder if I can live without it. Suddenly, while resisting the urge to stretch yet again, I see the most remarkable thing I have ever seen in my life. I notice a winged creature with the most amazing patterns and colors that I have ever seen. Colors that I didn't even know existed are all over this magical flying creature. I begin to wonder if there is any chance that after I shed my shell, I too may have wings and bright colors that the world could admire. For a moment I laugh at the thought and the silliness of my childish beliefs. What makes me think that I could become that from what I am now. As I begin to tire from the constant tug of war between me and my cocoon, I close my eyes and think ... What if I wake as a butterfly?

Reading those words helped me to know that I was on the path to following my purpose. I knew that those poetic words flowed through me because I was now able to own my own magic. With a sigh of relief and pleasure, I was able to put the pen down knowing that things were on the mend. That my next step would come. A new life was on the horizon.

Dream Bigger
– let your imagination go wild –

Then magic happened <u>again</u> in Texas. What is it with me and Texas? We were visiting my husband's family in San Antonio for the Christmas holidays. We were all having breakfast on the last day of our trip. My cell phone rang and I saw that it was Patricia.

Since the event, she and I had developed a deep friendship as we both expected we would. We had even traveled to see each other on several occasions. During those trips we discussed living out our mutual dream of creating a TV show. She and I both wanted that our whole lives. We even talked about creating one together! We discussed what kind of a show it would be. We would get super excited each time we had this conversation. We longed for it, but it never seemed to be quite the right time to actually do it. Does that sound familiar to a circumstance in your life?

She and I were so freaking intuitive with each other that when the phone rang I already had a

138

strange sense that it was about something important. I excused myself from the table and went into a different room to take the call. As soon as I answered the phone I heard her say, "Linda, let's do it. No more talking about it, no more wishing it, let's do our show."

The blood rushed to my head. My heart was racing. With 100% certainty and 0% doubt I replied with a resounding, "Hell to the yes!"

Just like that one of my dreams was becoming a reality. I was now a co-host and co-producer of a TV show! We spent all of 2019 working on this passion project. We named it *Soul Seekers TV* while on a group call when the creativity was flowing and that name came to us almost as a divine download. We have had the most incredible time watching our dream turn into a reality.

About six months later I made another decision. I thought that if I could make my tv show dream a reality, then what about the other things I really wanted to do? What about the book I have always wanted to write? Could I become an author and TV producer while still being in the classroom?

No more No's! This had been a mantra I was saying to myself. Thus, the only response that was
available about my book idea was - yes.

As I opened myself up for greater possibilities,
the divine downloads flowed through me day and
night. It was like I had turned on a faucet. I was
letting the flow drip into every area of my life.

When work is not aligned with you it feels hard
and tedious. Doing the work you are meant to do,
using the gifts you were given by Source, makes
the work seem fun. It gives me energy instead of
robbing it. After a day of working on my aligned
projects, I feel great instead of exhausted and
depleted.

If You Know Better, Do Better
– that's when it is time –

I used to tell my students all the time that once you know better, it is your responsibility to do better. I was the teacher that was known to notice a student drifting off into a daydream. I would always ask them to come to my desk and share with me about the thoughts they were having. It never failed, that until they became used to the question, they thought it was a discipline trap. They would try to convince me it was nothing, fearing that trouble was around the corner. But as a teacher, I knew their dreams had meaning. Until they could acknowledge and release those thoughts, I did not stand a chance of teaching them anything.

Then one day the lesson was reflected back to me. Sometimes the student is the greatest teacher of all. A student was at my desk and actually excited that I wanted to hear all about his daydream. He giggled as he gave an honest rendition of imagining that he was the one who had solved the mystery of Roanoke. He told me his theory on what he thought happened that caused the population to disappear. In his imaginary story he was interviewed by a news channel and was being asked to share his findings.

We had been learning about imagination, and he was using his beautifully. I was genuinely excited. The class and I turned his daydream into reality by pretending to be a news crew doing a story on his discovery. It was one of my greatest teaching days of all time.

At the end of the school day he ran to me for a hug before fleeing the classroom. He looked up at me and said, "Wow, isn't it fun to live out your dreams?!" Well, well, well...that unexpectedly hit me like a brick. He left the room just in time to avoid my blubbering sobs.

Yes, it is nice to live out our dreams. At that moment I realized that I had not been taking my own advice. I knew better, but I wasn't doing better! I did love teaching, but I wanted other things too.

From my earliest memories and journal entries, I can now see the pattern of wanting to help people and to be a teacher, writer, producer, and creator. I spent decades wishing it would "happen" for me. Yet all along, I was already on my path to my greatness. Unbeknownst to me, through all of my careers and experiences, I was amassing quite a bank of knowledge. It was time to start using it to be of service to others on their journey.

I had been living my days so absorbed in the lack mindset and grind that I did not have the ability to zoom out and see the bigger picture. All of the things that I really wanted were already on their way. I wish I had a time machine so that I could go back to that day and tell myself that everything was going to turn out OK. It would have saved me countless hours of stress and anxiety.

I started my reboot only knowing what was not working in my life. I was so unhappy and so aware of what was broken, that I was finally forced to start looking at why. My unhappiness was not outside, it was inside. My beliefs about myself made me feel terrible. Because I felt terrible, I was taking no action.

Even reflecting back as I write this, I have done so much work. It makes me smile to realize that

I have taught myself to love me all over again - piece by piece. I was starting to remember that no matter what was happening around me, loving myself was the single most important thing that I had to do to become my own beacon of light in the big dark sea of life.

I then made the honest decision to allow myself to express my creativity. It was time to go for it. With all of my self-love work, I was starting to know that my unique gifts could actually be used to monetize my life. I started to step more and more into my dream life each day because it felt exciting.

I could no longer live hiding from everything that made me happy for fear that I would be judged. I mean, shit, judgment will come no matter what choices I make. So I realized that the choices that fueled my desires were the most important choices of all.

Welcome Back To Your Authentic Self

– you have been missed –

I am writing this final chapter of the book years after that awful night in my backyard. I'm sitting at the desk of my home office. What a life reboot I've been through!

The magic that I created for myself through my reboot keeps on happening as I say, "Yes!" to things I'm excited about. So many other things have happened as a result. I have since taken a leave of absence from teaching. I am now working from home full time to author and publish this book. I am continuing the Soul Seeker's TV journey with my best friend Patricia Riberio Wolfson. We've already created and launched our first season of the show and are working on season two. I am also launching an online business to motivate and empower women who are stuck in their own mess and want to reboot into the life of their dreams.

As I write this, things have come full circle. Even as I click the keys to put these words on the page, I am looking out my window into the same backyard where I spun out of control. I am looking at the spot where I realized I had lost my spirit and identity, and I thought I had lost my husband.

Now, as I look at the spot where I railed against my husband, I actually have a smile on my face. As I think back through all that's happened in my own life reboot, I am filled with deep gratitude for the lowest point of my life. That may sound crazy to be grateful for it, but it's very true. That low point led me on a hero's journey to the present moment. I am doing the work, and serving in ways I have always dreamed.

I am reminded of the moment in this very backyard when I begged my husband to see me for who I was and love me as I am. I didn't believe then that he did. I didn't believe that we could ever get back to a place of love and compassion with one another. I was wrong.

Yesterday I received a belated birthday gift in the mail. My husband ordered it from abroad and it had finally arrived. It was the most beautiful gift I could have ever received. It was an engraved leather bound journal. The cover said the following:

> Linda, never forget that I love you. If I could give you one thing in life, I would give you the ability to see yourself through my eyes. Only then would you realize how special you are to me. Love, Tex

When I unwrapped it, I was stunned. Of all the things on the planet this man could have bought me, he actually gifted me with the most important thing of all...an acknowledgement. He could see me. He told me that I mattered. I was holding it in my hand, but reality didn't set in for a while. My tears, of course, did. This was absolutely amazing. My marriage had literally come full circle.

I had been through a full Life Reboot, and my life had survived it. I had my marriage back, stronger than ever. I had my self confidence back, and people were noticing. I knew who I was and what I was meant to do in this world. Now I can teach my daughter, and many, many other women how to step into their greatness. Because I've been through a life reboot, I can help her and others begin to navigate the waters of their souls to fully align to what each of us is meant to be in this world. Always by choice.

Write Your Reboot
– journal about turning it back on to reboot–

- What are your greatest talents and skills and how can you use them to evolve?
- How will you commit to taking better care of yourself?
- What kind of a legacy do you want to leave?
- What would you do if you knew you could not fail?
- What are your biggest takeaways from this book?

Final Thoughts

I hope that following the journey through my own life reboot has helped you to think about your own. My hope is that you have seen yourself in my stories and that it has illuminated the places where you need a shift in your life. I honor the path you've taken and all of the roads that have led you to read this book. I honor your path ahead as you forge forward with confidence and self-love.

At any point in time you have the power to reset and start anew. Sometimes, a reboot might be as easy as a walk on the beach or as bold as a weekend away. No matter what it looks like for you, take the time to make space in your heart and mind. Make your hopes and dreams a priority.

Again, I am so grateful that life has brought us together through this book. I invite you to a community of people just like you who are working to shift and reboot their lives. It is a loving space, with even more resources to help you through your reboot. I know how important it is to have community around you while you make shifts in your life. The name of the Facebook Group is called Life Reboot by Linda Krauss Barnett. Join us. My website is www.lindakraussbarnett.com. You can find additional information about how to contact me, and how to dive deeper into your own life reboot.

Just remember, when you feel yourself in a tailspin, turn it off, wait, and then gently turn it back on again and wait for your system to reboot.

About The Author

Relying on her career as an educator and her passion as a writer, Linda Krauss Barnett has been able to reboot her life from one of doubt and despair to one filled with passion, purpose, and self-love. She is helping women to redefine what is possible at any stage of their journey by trusting in the power of their inner warrior and creating lives aligned with their dreams.

She's living the life of which she has always dreamed. She is proud of realizing her life-long desire of becoming an author through this debut book and is also a co-host/co-producer of *Soul Seekers TV* w/Patricia Ribiero Wolfson.